FARMER PARTICIPATORY RESEARCH

Rhetoric and reality

Christine Okali, James Sumberg and
John Farrington

INTERMEDIATE TECHNOLOGY PUBLICATIONS
on behalf of the
OVERSEAS DEVELOPMENT INSTITUTE
1994

Intermediate Technology Publications
103–105 Southampton Row, London WC1B 4HH, UK

© Overseas Development Institute 1994

ISBN 1 85339 252 9

Typeset by ODI and Dorwyn Ltd, Rowlands Castle, Hants
Printed by SRP, Exeter

Contents

ACRONYMS

ADRO	Western Region Development Association (Honduras)
ATA	Appropriate Technology Association (Thailand)
ATIP	Agricultural Technology Improvement Project (Botswana)
BAIF	Bharatiya Agri-Industries Foundation (India)
BARI	Bangladesh Agricultural Research Institute
BRAC	Bangladesh Rural Advancement Committee
CAAP	Andean Centre for Popular Action (Ecuador)
CARE	An international NGO
CATT	Research and Training Centre for Tropical Agronomy (Costa Rica)
CESA	Centre for Agricultural Services
CG	Consultative Group (same as CGIAR)
CGIAR	Consultative Group for International Agricultural Research
CIAT	International Centre for Tropical Agriculture (Colombia)
CIMMYT	International Centre for Maize and Wheat Improvement
CIPRES	Centre for Research, Promotion and Rural and Social Development (Nicaragua)
CRS	Catholic Relief Services
CRSP	Cooperative Research Support Programme
DELTA	Development Education Leadership Teams
ENDA	Environment and Development Activities (Zimbabwe)
FBU	United Brethren Foundation (Ecuador)
FIVBD	Friends in Village Development (Bangladesh)
GRAAP	Groupe de Recherche et d'Appui pour l'Autopromotion Paysanne
ICIPIE	International Centre for Insect Physiology and Ecology
ICLARM	International Centre for Living Aquatic Resources Management
ICRISAT	International Crops Research Institute for the Semi-Arid Tropics
IDS	Institute of Development Studies
IIED	International Institute for Environment and Development
LEIA	Information Centre for Low External Input and Sustainable Agriculture
IPRA	Participatory Research in Agriculture Project, CIAT
ISAR	Agricultural Research Institute (Rwanda)
ISNAR	International Service for National Agricultural Research
ITDG	Intermediate Technology Development Group
MCC	Mennonite Central Committee
NDUAT	Narendra Dev University of Agriculture and Technology
NRI	Natural Resources Institute
ODI	Overseas Development Institute
OFCOR	On-farm Client Oriented Research
PIP	Production for Production Research (Ecuador)
PRA	Participative Rural Appraisal
PRADAN	Professional Assistance for Development Action (India)
PRATEC	Proyecto Andino de Tecnologias Campesinas
PTD	Participative Technology Development
PVO/NGO-NRMS	Private Voluntary Organizations/Non-governmental Organizations Natural Resources Support Programme (USA)
RDRS	Rangpur Dinajpur Rural Services (Bangladesh)
RRA	Rapid Rural Appraisal
SWOT	Strengths, Weaknesses, Opportunities and Threats
UAPPI	The Union of Associations of Producers and Processors of Yuca
USAID	United States Agency for International Development

Preface

This study grew out of a realization in 1990 that the 'participatory' agricultural research projects we had been involved in designing and advising would one day need to be seriously evaluated. Thus, we began with a very practical goal: to develop and test monitoring and evaluation strategies and tools that would be useful in the context of similar farmer participatory research projects.

Two insights quickly followed. First, there was reason to believe that the kinds of indicators commonly used to assess the impact of agricultural research, such as rate of technology adoption and changes in production and productivity, would be of limited value in the marginal agricultural environments in which much farmer participatory research takes place. In addition, these indicators would tell us little about the other, non-technical, objectives often associated with farmer participatory research. Second, the literature and experience concerning farmer participation in agricultural research had expanded rapidly over the last several years. This now considerable body of work was being fed both by the experience of individuals and organizations implementing activities in the field, as well as by lively theoretical and ideological debates relating to issues such as participation, knowledge and empowerment.

Thus we decided that the original objective might best be approached through a detailed and critical review of the field experience and the related theoretical discussion. This volume is that review. It attempts to lay out the now vast and varied field of farmer participatory research by exploring objectives and actual implementation strategies, and a range of associated issues. The review has not resulted in concrete guidelines for monitoring and evaluating farmer participatory research. Rather, we present a conceptual framework that may be useful as a basis for designing, monitoring and evaluating agricultural research at the collegiate interface. The further development and field testing of this framework is the object of a continuing effort.

We were most fortunate to have had financial support from the British Overseas Development Administration and CARE (through the

vii

PVO/NGO–NRMS Support Project) for this research. We are grateful for this support and only hope that the analysis presented here will help these and other organizations develop, fund, implement and evaluate more effective activities.

A number of individuals contributed directly to this study, including the staff of the ODI Library who were helpful in identifying and making available a large body of useful material. We are grateful to those members of the ODI Agricultural Administration (Research and Extension) Network who responded to our request for documentation and those who agreed to be interviewed about specific project activities or issues. Others were most generous with unpublished documentation, and the case study material in Chapter 4 reflects this generosity. Several months into the work we held a seminar in London, which was valuable in orientating and clarifying our approach. Finally, we profited from discussions with colleagues, a number of whom also reviewed earlier drafts of this volume. The contributions of Stephen Biggs, David Gibbon, Elon Gilbert and Louise Sperling deserve special mention.

CHRISTINE OKALI
JAMES SUMBERG
JOHN FARRINGTON

NORWICH
APRIL 1994

1 Introduction

Background and objectives

THIS STUDY IS about an idea which, over the last ten years, has become the centrepiece of a worldwide movement. The original idea was simple enough: a greater degree of farmer involvement would make agricultural research in the developing world more effective. The movement that has developed around this idea is, however, far from simple. Rather, it is characterized by and associated with a series of debates around topics such as knowledge, participation, empowerment, local organization and the comparative advantage of different research and development institutions. The rapidly expanding literature that embodies these debates is a manifestation of the level of interest in both the theory and practice of what has come to be called farmer participatory research.

The purpose of this study is to review and evaluate recent developments, both in terms of concepts and implementation, in farmer participatory research. The review forms part of a wider research project to develop monitoring and evaluation strategies, tools and indicators for assessing the impact of farmer participatory research projects and activities. It follows on from work by Farrington and Martin (1987; 1990) as well as subsequent reviews and analyses of farmer participation in agricultural research detailed below.

The objective is to review farmer participatory research primarily as a process through which agricultural technology[1] is developed and evaluated. As such we start with the understanding that farmer participatory research is, *a priori*, neither more nor less valuable than any other approach to agricultural research. It is simply part of a continuum of research approaches, the extremes of which reflect, to a greater and lesser degree, formal and informal research processes and institutions. Thus, this review does not set out to advocate for the expanded use of farmer participatory research, but rather to discover how the approach has

---

[1] For this review, agricultural technology is understood in its broadest sense: it encompasses plant varieties and animal breeds, farming practices and agricultural production and processing tools, in addition to specific mental constructs, cultural codes and forms of management and co-operation.

1

been and is being applied, to identify its key distinguishing features and to assess in what way its potential value might be enhanced. Throughout the review we are particularly concerned with programmes that have developed, or are attempting to move toward, more 'collegiate' modes of interaction (Biggs, 1989).

Farmer participatory research is understood by many to be one element of a larger 'participatory' development agenda which aims not only to generate, test and disseminate technologies, but also to change the orientation of existing research and development structures, develop a sustainable, community-based research capability, and create new social and political institutions. Thus, while participatory development programmes and activities as a whole are not the focus of the review, they are one part of the framework within which farmer participatory research is being discussed and carried out and they are, therefore, an important element of our analysis.

We are acutely aware that innovations come from a number of different sources, including farmers, and that many agricultural producers actively seek, test and pass on new ideas, techniques and materials. Indeed, these two propositions form the dominant backdrop for farmer participatory research. A major concern for this study, therefore, is to determine how farmer participatory research programmes conceive of and interact with the farmers' own research. One goal is to discover the factors affecting both the productivity and sustainability of these interactions.

Another important element of farmer participatory research is the role which non-governmental organizations are playing in both its conception and its implementation. While some non-governmental organizations have historically been active in the field of agricultural research, this is a new activity for the majority. The Overseas Development Institute's recently completed studies of the relations between non-government development organizations and state agricultural research institutions provide a detailed review of these activities (Farrington and Bebbington, 1993). The four volumes of the ODI study jointly cover 70 case studies and provide a valuable picture of the wide variation in orientation, objectives, and operational approaches among non-government organizations involved in participatory development.

The present study does not enter into, however, the debate over which types of organizations and institutions are better suited to participate in or lead certain aspects of the agricultural research process. There is now ample evidence of the significant heterogeneity in orientation and competence within the most commonly used institutional categories (national and international research institutions, non-governmental organizations etc.) to warrant serious reflection regarding the continued value of this line of debate. In fact, a central theme which emerges from our study is that the use of dichotomies (governmental or non-governmental; formal or informal; insider or outsider), that characterizes many aspects of the literature and discussion relating to farmer participatory research, has been a major factor hindering both clarity of concepts and effectiveness of implementation. We are, nevertheless, aware that a knowledge of specific administrative and institutional characteristics must be integrated into programme planning and implementation (Heinemann and Biggs, 1985).

The review also does not cover the large body of literature on institutional frameworks and mechanisms to promote better linkages between the range of actors involved in agricultural research and extension activities. These topics have been the subject of much recent writing, and are a major focus of the International Service for National Agricultural Research (ISNAR) (Merrill-Sands and Kaimowitz, 1990). It is clear, however, that all agricultural research, extension and development activities take place within a given (and potentially volatile) political, economic, institutional and agro-climatic context. The study is concerned, therefore, with the identification and analysis of these contextual factors as they affect farmer participatory research programmes, and these questions are addressed specifically in Chapters 6 and 8.

The remainder of this chapter consists of two sections. The first is a synopsis of the material and major arguments presented in the seven subsequent chapters. The second section indicates the major sources of information upon which our analysis was based.

The rhetoric and reality of farmer participatory research: a synopsis

The sub-title of this work reflects a telling contradiction within the broad body of writing and activity relating more or less directly to farmer participatory research. On the one hand there is a rich intellectual discussion that explores, among other things, the nature of knowledge, with particular emphasis on interaction and meaning at the interface between (formal and informal, local and non-local) knowledge systems. This discussion is epitomized by the work of Norman Long and his colleagues, and the title of their recently published work, *Battlefields of Knowledge: The Interlocking of Theory and Practice in Social Research and Development* reflects both the breadth and drama of the debate (Long and Long, 1992). In principle, farmer participatory research is centrally located within this large canvas of conflict and negotiation as it attempts to create a more fruitful interface between formal and informal agricultural research. The contradiction is that much of the activity of farmer participatory research programmes and projects comes down to

3

controlled experimental or test plots on which crop varieties or production techniques are demonstrated and evaluated. There is little drama, and despite the rhetoric of participation, little sense of negotiation. In fact, these particular interface situations look strikingly similar to the on-farm trials that were and continue to be the hallmark of the farming systems research. Thus, a central question that sits just below the surface of this study relates to this gap between the intellectual discussion and the field reality. We raise this issue, not to dispute the significance of on-farm experimentation and the value of enhanced farmer participation, but rather to pinpoint potential areas within the whole spectrum of what is referred to as farmer participatory research which appear to offer scope for further consideration and development.

The study begins with two chapters which provide a context within which a number of examples of farmer participatory research projects and activities will subsequently be examined. These contextual aspects are particularly important for a meaningful understanding of the current state of farmer participatory research. Specifically, the discussion about farmer participation in agricultural research has become a focal point for a number of debates, which take place at different levels and through different fora, involve different individuals and institutions, and have more or less a direct relation to the way in which farmer participatory research is implemented in the field. These debates are rooted in a wide range of disciplines and intellectual traditions, including sociology, anthropology, political science, geography, adult education and agronomy. At the same time they revolve around subjects that at once cut across these academic disciplines and form the touchstones of current development thinking: knowledge, participation, empowerment, sustainability, livelihoods, systems and institutions. We will argue that these debates, which have provided a complex (and at times contradictory) web of conceptual and theoretical underpinnings for farmer participatory research, have developed to such a level and have become so all-encompassing that they frequently bear little resemblance to farmer participatory research projects and activities in the field.

Thus, Chapter 2 (An Introduction to Farmer Participatory Research) provides a survey of the broad outlines of farmer participatory research. Two key principles are identified: farmers actively seek out and test new techniques and ideas (farmers' own research), and there is an important potential synergy through the interaction of formal agricultural research and farmers' own research. With a focus on poorer groups in more marginal environments, these principles are increasingly cited to justify a shift from other models of applied agricultural research to farmer participatory research.

However, the idea of farmers participating in agricultural research is not new, and indeed was an important theme in farming systems research.

4

While some proponents of farmer participatory research go to great lengths to distance it from farming systems research, in fact they share many common roots (the extent of these commonalities become more evident through the examples discussed in Chapters 4 and 5). While several frameworks which distinguish between various modes, levels or intensities of participation can be identified, it is clear that the appropriate form and level of interaction between farmers and agricultural researchers will vary depending on objectives, the specific technologies under study, and so on.

The chapter ends with a short discussion of the boundaries of farmer participatory research. We argue, as have others before us, that participatory research cannot be seen in isolation from other, non-participatory agricultural research activities, such as on-station research on the one hand, and farmers' own research on the other. Attention is then drawn to the question of whether, in practice, farmer participatory research will necessarily be any more effective than farming systems research, or any other type of agricultural research, in dealing with larger policy issues.

Some of these questions are explored in greater detail in Chapter 3 (Associated Themes and Concepts), as they are integral elements of the intellectual and political context in which and from which the interest in farmer participatory research emerged. While farmer participatory research has appeared relatively recently, most of the themes with which it is associated are not new, but form part of a historical shift in opinions and practice regarding rural development. It is important to recognize this contextual position of farmer participatory research and to see it, therefore, as another step in our understanding of development and change.

The recent history of interest in and attempts to increase farmers' involvement in agricultural research are explored initially. Increased farmer involvement was fundamental to the farming systems research movement, and most recent attempts to restructure national agricultural research institutions have emphasized participatory structures – which have included farmers – to foster more decentralized decision-making. Most farming systems research programmes were, and are, implemented largely through research institutions, while farmer participatory research is implemented through a wider range of institutions. Nevertheless, farming systems research and farmer participatory research share many common frameworks and activities, and current farmer participatory research projects must be analysed in this light, bearing in mind the considerable experience already gained.

Closely related to the discussion of participation is the prominence given to the concept of 'empowerment' in much of the literature concerning farmer participatory research, evidence that a group of broad social and political goals have become closely associated with the concept of farmer participatory research. This is due, in part, to the fact that much farmer participatory research takes place within the context of development activities. And in line with these broader trends, development organizations including non-governmental organizations play a more central role in the discussion and implementation of farmer participatory research than they did relative to farming systems research. While farmer participatory research has been associated with the empowerment agenda at a number of levels, from decision-making about research to more profound changes in power relations, there is a certain gap between this discussion and the actual nature and focus of many project activities. At the point of implementation, the empowerment agenda is often addressed by establishing or strengthening farmer organizations, which then frequently becomes the avenue for the implementing crop trials.

The interest in farmer participatory research cannot be disassociated from the increased awareness of and respect for indigenous or local knowledge. Research has focused on the nature and structure of local knowledge and knowledge systems, highlighting differences and similarities between local and non-local, insider and outsider, and formal and informal knowledge, as well as attempting to identify local categories and taxonomies. Of major interest for farmer participatory research is the interface of local knowledge, experience and experimental skills and more formal agricultural research. The question of differences within communities in terms of interest, knowledge, skills and innovative behaviour has important implications for the implementation of farmer participatory research. While this question relates directly to the earlier discussion of empowerment, these individual differences, and the factors determining them, have not featured prominently in the farmer participatory research literature. This lacuna is particularly important in the light of the group or community approach to implementation that is being taken by some programmes.

Another important element of the context is the increasing interest in low input, sustainable production systems. With a focus on poor people in marginal environments and the backdrop of the wider empowerment agenda mentioned earlier, there is now an explicit understanding among many promoters and practitioners that farmer participatory research has clear advantages for the development of appropriate, environmentally friendly and sustainable production systems. As previously noted, however, this view is simplistic in that it tends to overlook social and ecological diversity, and the implications these have for local livelihood strategies.

The final section of Chapter 3 introduces some of the key methods which are associated with farmer participatory research. Attention is drawn to the debate regarding the relative merits of quantitative and qualitative methods, and the implications of different methods for both participation and empowerment. Part of this debate relates to the widespread promotion of the tools and techniques commonly associated with Participatory Rural Appraisal (PRA). Another key area of discussion, which has very clear links to the farming systems research experience, is the use and form of field trials. These questions are central to our overall analysis of farmer participatory research.

Chapter 4 (Farmer Participatory Research in Practice) examines in some detail a selection of on-going programmes focused on or involving farmer participatory research. First, an overall framework which divides the examples into four groups along two axes is proposed. The first axis contrasts farmer participatory research activities which take place within what are primarily agricultural research programmes with those taking place within broader development programmes or projects. The available material makes clear that many farmer participatory research activities take place within more general development projects and relatively few projects are involved solely in farmer participatory research. In addition, agricultural research, and farmer participatory research specifically, absorbs a relatively small proportion of the resources of most implementing organizations and projects, few of which have staff with significant training or experience in research.

The second axis distinguishes between programmes and activities involving more or less active and direct intervention. Some projects put major emphasis on training to improve, strengthen or formalize farmers' experimental skills, while others essentially feed ideas or material into existing informal research processes.

The presentation is divided into two parts. The first covers farmer participatory research taking place within general development programmes, and is almost entirely based on the recently published ODI study of NGO activities. The second part reviews a selection of specific cases of farmer participatory research that were designed primarily as, or take place within, agricultural research programmes. The cases include a range of geographical locations, institutions and strategies. The concern is to identify approaches and activities which can be clearly distinguished from those typically associated with farming systems research. As many participatory research activities include on-farm trials implemented through groups, different approaches to farmer organization are highlighted.

A focus on the type and level of project intervention stems from the first principle of farmer participatory research: the existence, importance and potential of farmers' own research. While this point figures prominently in much of the writing about farmer participatory research, many projects actually stimulate, strengthen or enhance farmers' own research through training in trial design, management and analysis. These practical efforts to add a more systematic and 'scientific' base to farmers' own research are somewhat ironic – not only do they indicate a basic lack of confidence in local skills, but they also fly in the face of another important sub-theme of the discussion of farmer participatory research in the literature – the narrowness and false objectivity of the scientific method (these concerns are examined in greater detail in Chapter 6).

Chapter 5 (Key Issues in Implementation) addresses a number of critical questions which are common to many programmes. These include the selection of participants, the sustainability of the investigatory process, the implementation of an agro-ecological perspective, the effects on research agendas and finally, the information needed prior to project implementation. While farmer participatory research, along with other participatory approaches, is aimed at the larger rural community, it is not possible for everyone to participate in the activities. Thus, all programmes face the question of how to select participants. The critical decision is how to reconcile concerns about breadth of participation and equity with practical and robust research design. Where research is focused on technology development, selection criteria often stress research capabilities or skills, whereas in programmes designed to enhance long-term processes within communities, representational concerns tend to dominate.

Related to this question of who participates is the concern with farmer organization. Among development agencies it is widely accepted that individuals can only affect the underlying problems determining their situation by being organized. The reasons used to justify this focus on organizing are examined from the perspective of farmer participatory research. While the empowerment agenda is central, there are also other, more pragmatic considerations such as the ability to impact on a larger group of farmers, the ability to engage in a meaningful dialogue and the very nature of specific technologies. What is significant is the fact that many programmes initiate new groups rather than build on existing organizations.

The creation of a sustainable process of innovation at the level of communities is the objective of the majority of programmes taking a larger development perspective, and is addressed in a number of ways. Great care is taken by some, for example, to minimize possible dependence on the project. A general lack of understanding of local processes of experimentation and innovation means, however, that projects are poorly placed to address the complex question of sustainability.

At another level, the sustainability of technical initiatives is addressed more or less actively by all client-oriented research programmes. Organizations involved with farmer participatory research have, as previously noted, generally aligned themselves with the call for an alternative agricultural development agenda, and the 'agro-ecological' approach has been often cited as being particularly appropriate. However, apart from the ICLARM examples, the experience to date with the implementation of this alternative agenda is not particularly encouraging. In some cases where the association with agro-ecological concerns is seen to be part of a specific strategy of an organization or movement to define a separate identity, there is even potential conflict between programmes and clients. In any case, since results are unlikely to appear in the short term, it is difficult to see how these objectives can be achieved within a project context.

At this point, the chapter moves on to a discussion of research policy. One of the key criticisms of farming systems research was its lack of attention to policy issues and this is, therefore, regarded by many as an important objective of farmer participatory research. The chapter concludes with a discussion of the information needed prior to programme implementation. From the material reviewed, and focusing on specific types of programmes, we identify four categories of information which would seem to be vital for successful programme planning: institutions and patterns of social and economic relations; farmer experimentation; the flow of resources and information; and gaps in local technical knowledge. The review suggests that the first three of these categories are seldom investigated in any formal manner. The attention given to the fourth reflects the centrality of indigenous knowledge in the whole discussion of participatory research and development.

Chapter 6 (Analysis of Current Trends and Practice) provides an initial assessment of the impact of Farmer Participatory Research and any shifts towards more collegiate interaction between formal and informal research. First, the examples presented in Chapters 4 and 5 are linked with the earlier discussion of the conceptual and methodological underpinnings (Chapters 2 and 3). Particular approaches to farmer participatory research and particular stages in a research programme are identified that appear to offer greatest potential benefits from both the farmers' and researchers' viewpoint. It is argued that different levels of farmer and researcher participation are likely to be appropriate in different contexts and with different types of research being undertaken. Subsequently, two of the most common participatory activities, problem identification and on-farm trials, are evaluated in the same way. The chapter ends with a further assessment of the technological agendas commonly associated with farmer participatory research.

Chapter 7 (Monitoring and Evaluation) addresses the issue of the monitoring and evaluation of farmer participatory research activities. The chapter begins with an analysis of experiences with monitoring and evaluation identified during the review. Attention is drawn again to the wide variety of programmes included under the umbrella of farmer participatory research and their different monitoring and evaluation needs. Reference is made to the ways in which farmer participatory research activities are being evaluated, and gaps in monitoring and evaluation over the whole continuum of participatory research are identified. The lack of a substantial basis for the evaluation of programme activities at the collegiate interface is identified as a key constraint to the further advancement of farmer participatory research at this end of the continuum.

Finally, in Chapter 8 (Future Directions: linking evaluation indicators to project design) we propose a framework and methodology to identify and characterize farmers' own research and information exchange. It is argued that further development of this framework will facilitate both better project design and the development of meaningful monitoring and evaluation strategies.

Sources

The literature relating to farmer participatory research can be divided into four major blocks. The first deals with a broad range of theoretical and institutional issues; the second reports actual field experience; the third block consists of reviews and synthesis documents, and the fourth, often in the form of manuals, focuses more narrowly on participatory research methods.

During the last five years there has been a tremendous increase in documentation relating to farmer participatory research and particularly reports of actual field experience. These have resulted partly in response to calls from various organizations including the Institute of Development Studies (IDS), the Information Centre for Low External Input and Sustainable Agriculture (ILEIA) and the International Institute for Environmental Development (IIED), and the related increase in 'grey literature' outlets. Particular emphasis has been placed on documenting participatory processes.

This explosion in written material, and the new field activity upon which much of it is based, must also be seen in relation to several key events and documents. The edited volume by Brokensha *et al.* (1980) on *Indigenous Knowledge Systems and Development* and the 1978 workshop on 'The Use of Indigenous Technical Knowledge' held at the IDS, raised most of the issues which would be regarded by many to be part of the justification for farmer participatory research. A number of the papers from this meeting later appeared in a special issue of the Bulletin of the Institute of Development Studies (IDS) under the title *Rural Development: Whose Knowledge Counts?* (IDS, 1979). There is a large body of associated writing on the subject of indigenous technical knowledge, which was recently reviewed by Fairhead (1992). Other more

10

recent work was presented at the IDS workshop 'Beyond Farmer First: Rural Peoples' Knowledge, Agricultural Research and Extension Practice' held in October, 1992. The objective of this workshop was to develop strategies for enhancing effective and equitable partnerships between indigenous and formal knowledge systems.

Farrington and Martin's (1987) review of farmer participatory research, which was updated in 1990, has already been cited. This review was prepared as a background paper for the 1987 IDS workshop entitled 'Farmers and Agricultural Research: Complementary Methods', which resulted in a collection of papers published in a special issue of *Experimental Agriculture* (Farming Systems Series 10, 1988, Vol. 24: 269 –342) and a widely distributed volume – *Farmer First* – edited by Chambers *et al.* (1989). This workshop was followed in 1988 by another meeting held at Leusden under the auspices of the Information Centre for Low External Input and Sustainable Agriculture (ILEIA) on the subject of 'Operational Approaches for Participative Technology Development in Sustainable Agriculture' (ILEIA, 1989) and the theme of sustainable agriculture now forms a substantial component of the farmer participatory research literature (e.g., Hiemstra *et al.*, 1992). Since 1987 there has, therefore, been a steady stream of workshops and conferences focused on farmer participatory research, and these have been a major factor in the increase in written material (e.g., Scherr, 1991; Scoones and Thompson, 1992). Most of the material from the earlier workshops is included in Amanor's annotated bibliography (Amanor, 1990).

Other key channels for materials relating to farmer participatory research (and the closely related field of farming systems research) include publications of the ODI's Agricultural Administration (Research and Extension) Network, the *ILEIA Newsletter*, the various regional farming systems research networks, the more recent annual meetings of the Association for Farming Systems Research and Extension (and the associated *Journal for Farming Systems Research–Extension*), and IIED's Sustainable Agriculture Programme.

Another major source was the ODI case studies of participatory research and development experience by government and voluntary agencies (Bebbington and Thiele [1993] on Latin and Central America; Farrington and Lewis [1993] on Asia; and Wellard and Copestake [1993] on Africa), and three additional documents which look at the relationship between non-government and government organizations (Farrington and Bebbington, 1991; Bebbington and Farrington, 1992 and 1993). These documents explore in detail various scenarios for co-operation between government and voluntary organizations in the realm of agricultural research.

In addition to the review of farmer participatory research concepts and practice by Farrington and Martin, Amanor's annotated bibliography is a key document (almost one-third of the entries in this bibliography are from the Farming Systems Symposium in Florida in 1986, the 1987 workshop 'Farmers and Agricultural Researchers: Complementary Methods' and the 1988 ILEIA meeting on 'Operational Approaches to Participatory Technology Development in Sustainable Development'. More recently several reviews and summaries have been prepared either entirely or partly under the auspices of ILEIA, including *Joining Farmers' Experiments: Experiences in participatory technology development* edited by Haverkort *et al.*, (1991) and *Developing Tools Together: Report of a study on the role of participation in the development of tools, equipment and techniques in appropriate technology programmes*' (van der Bliek and Veldhuizen, 1993).

The literature on research methods has also increased significantly. Building on the earlier conference on 'Rapid Rural Appraisal' (RRA) held in Khon Kaen, Thailand in 1985 (KKU, 1987), IIED has played a significant role in the promotion of Rapid Rural Appraisal (RRA) and Participatory Rural Appraisal (PRA) techniques through its publication of *RRA Notes*. In addition, there are a number of training manuals and other on-farm research materials for practitioners which have recently been reviewed in *On-farm Research: An annotated bibliography* (Clinch, 1994).

Apart from these materials, there is a vast body of unpublished and particularly valuable project proposals, reports, and evaluations, an impressive selection of which is available in the ODI library. Finally, the study is based on information received from a general mailing to ODI network members which called for experiences not previously published. In some cases more focused correspondence and discussion followed which highlighted particular concerns and issues that the projects were trying to resolve. Programmes for detailed study were selected in consultation with collaborating institutions and organizations and include some with which we have had previous involvement.

It is clear that the material reviewed probably represents a small proportion of the total information relating to the practice of farmer participatory research, even though we used ODI's extensive network to contact field researchers. While much information never emerges from the field, an attempt was made to meet with practitioners and make contact with ODI Network members. While incomplete, the review covers the major themes running through the farmer participatory research literature and it gives a reasonable view of the present state of knowledge and experience.

2 An Introduction to Farmer Participatory Research

RESEARCH CAN BE defined as careful study or investigation, especially in order to discover new facts or information. There are many classifications of types of research activity, and various attempts have been made to identify steps or stages in the research process. For the purposes of this study a very general framework that accommodates a wide range of individual and institutional involvement in what we will consider agricultural research is needed. Thus research, whether formal or informal and involving scientists or farmers, will be considered to be a more or less deliberate and systematic process that proceeds through three general stages: (i) identification of opportunities (perhaps more commonly referred to as problems or constraints), (ii) identification of ideas or options and (iii) testing and/or adaptation of the ideas and options.

While at one level of discussion farmer participatory research is seen as an easily identifiable and well-defined research approach, a careful reading of the literature quickly demonstrates the contrary. In practice the term is used to encompass a wide variety of research and research-related activities. In fact, the term farmer participatory research is often used synonymously with other terms such as Participatory Technology Development (Haverkort *et al.*, 1991; ETC, 1992), Agricultural Technology Development (Farrington and Bebbington, 1993) and Appropriate Technology (van der Bliek and van Veldhuizen, 1993). At the same time, the actual research objectives and activities discussed under these various titles are closely related to other on-farm, client-oriented research approaches including farming systems research.

In some cases, therefore, farmer participatory research describes projects designed simply to carry out research in close collaboration with farmers, while in others it refers to research activities carried out within a much broader agricultural research framework, which in some cases actually includes extension activities and institutions. The term is also used to refer to activities which lie within, but are subsidiary to, broader development programmes focused on, for example, community organization, education or water. This is part of the explanation of why the discussion of farmer participatory research is intertwined with wider

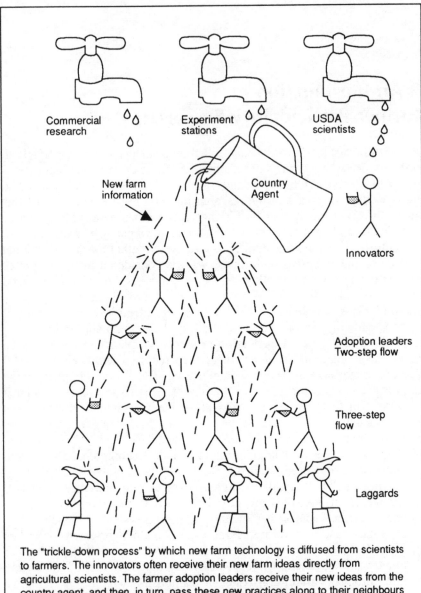

Commercial research

Experiment stations

USDA scientists

New farm information

Country Agent

Innovators

Adoption leaders
Two-step flow

Three-step flow

Laggards

The "trickle-down process" by which new farm technology is diffused from scientists to farmers. The innovators often receive their new farm ideas directly from agricultural scientists. The farmer adoption leaders receive their new ideas from the country agent, and then, in turn, pass these new practices along to their neighbours and friends. Research studies indicate, however that the new ideas often do not trickle down all the way to the low-income laggards. And the new technical information may not be as accurate as when it was first passed along by the country agent.

Figure 2.1 *Classical depiction of the diffusion process in the context of a central source of innovation model.* Source: Rogers (1960)

debates about empowerment,[1] social justice and community development. In some ways, therefore, and for some institutions and individuals, the focus of farmer participatory research is as much on political, social and institutional processes as on the development and testing of agricultural technology. These alternative views of farmer participatory research relate to Richards' (1989b) distinction between 'demand-side populism' (the promotion of interests and claims by social groups from below) and 'supply-side populism' (the promotion, by 'progressive' outsiders, of self-improvement and self-organization among the poor and weak).

In terms of a technological focus, farmer participatory research is being used to investigate a wide range of agricultural problems including both production and processing. Some authors have argued that it has particular value for investigating 'agro-ecological' 'low-input' and 'sustainable' production systems (Chambers and Jiggins, 1986; Chambers *et al.*, 1989; Woodhouse, 1991; Reijntjes *et al.*, 1992).

The first principle of farmer participatory research is an assumption that many farmers are actively engaged in an on-going search for new or improved crop planting material, varieties and production techniques, and livelihood options more generally. The documentation of the existence and diversity of 'farmers' own research' is now well-known (e.g., Johnson, 1972; Biggs, 1980; Brammer, 1980; Richards, 1986; Abedin and Haque, 1987). As will become apparent, there are important differences between this vision of 'research-minded' farmers as generators of new information, understanding and technology, and Roger's 'innovators' who are perhaps more appropriately termed 'first adopters' (Rogers, 1962). According to Rogers, what distinguishes innovators from early adopters is *direct* access to scientists and research results. There is no suggestion, however, that the innovators themselves are, or can be, a source of new understanding or technology (Figure 2.1).

Another principle is that there are elements within local farming systems and the larger contexts within which they exist which have not been observed or examined by formal research, but which are understood and are being explored by farmers themselves. The key assumption is that it is through an examination of these elements, an examination based on the knowledge and understanding of both farmers and researchers, that sustainable techniques and solutions can be developed. Thus, in principle, farmer participatory research aims to operate at the interface between knowledge systems: it can be described as a people-centred process of purposeful and creative interplay between local individuals and communities on the one hand, and outsiders with formal agricultural and

---

[1] In the sense of 'the creation of an environment of inquiry in which people question and resist structural reasons for their poverty, through learning and action' (Cromwell and Wiggins, 1993, p.91).

research knowledge on the other (i.e., a collegiate interface).

All agricultural research is or should be carried out with specific clients or potential end-users in view. Although many programmes of farmer participatory research attempt to work with whole rural communities rather than individuals, in line with an overall poverty focus, most projects emphasize the involvement of the poorest members and particularly women. The clients of farmer participatory research, therefore, are generally identified as low-income rural people who may be fully occupied with agricultural production or agriculturally related activities, or may have alternative income sources outside the agricultural sector. Not only is this research approach considered to be especially appropriate for working with the rural poor, but it is also seen to be essential for working in areas which might be considered 'difficult', fragile, and demonstrating low potential for agricultural production.[2] These environments are characterized by low, unreliable rainfall, poor and easily degradable soils, hilly topographies, and are more often than not isolated from centres of communication, services and trade (Amanor, 1990). The most frequently cited cases are the Andean region of Latin America, the semi-arid zones of Africa and tribal areas of Asia.[3] While these are perhaps the extreme examples, they do highlight the more general characteristics of poor rural areas, including a limited range of non-agricultural income opportunities, high rates of out-migration and often substantial distances from services, including those of formal agricultural research and extension.

Many descriptions of the locations where farmer participatory research is being implemented emphasize their diversity, with the implication that standardized or blanket solutions are unlikely to succeed. In the main, farmer participatory research is being popularized as a means to redress the perceived imbalance in the focus of formal agricultural research, which is seen to have concentrated on high potential areas with more reliable rainfall regimes and access to markets and communications.[4]

While these are the commonly understood reference points for farmer participatory research, there has been no generally accepted statement of

---

[2] Some researchers do argue that farmer participatory research should be valuable in a much wider range of situations and circumstances.

[3] It must be noted that not all authors agree that marginal or low potential areas are so easily identified. Biggs and Farrington (1991a) have argued that a number of these areas have potential for substantial increases in productivity. PRATEC (1991), has argued along the same lines for the Andean region, Gubbels (1992a) for the Sub-Sahel. Mellor (1988) on the other hand has pointed out that poverty occurs equally in areas of low and high agricultural potential and is, at least in part, structurally determined.

[4] Röling (1988) points out that this is also true of extension. With reference to Kenya, he demonstrates that good extension workers are stationed in areas where agriculture is more developed, otherwise farmers complain.

Table 2.1 Physical, social and economic conditions for research stations, resource-rich and resource-poor farms

Characteristic	Research station	Resource-rich farms	Resource-poor farms
Soils	Deep and fertile, few constraints	Few effective constraints	Shallow, infertile, often serve constraints
Macro and micro nutrient deficiencies	Rare Remedial	Occasional	Quite common
Plot size and nature	Large, square	Large	Small, irregular
Hazards	Nil or few	Few, usually controllable	More common – floods, droughts, animals grazing crops, etc
Irrigation	Usually available	Usually available	Often non-existent
Size of management unit	Large, contiguous	Large or medium, contiguous	Small, often scattered and fragmented
Natural vegetation	Eliminated	Eliminated or highly controlled	Used or controlled at micro-level
Access to purchased inputs	Unlimited, reliable	High, reliable	Low, unreliable
Source of seed	Foundation stocks and breeders' seed of high quality	Purchased, high quality	Own seed
Access to credit when needed	Unlimited	Good access	Poor access and seasonal shortages of cash when most needed
Irrigation, where facilities exist	Fully controlled by research station	Controlled by farmers or by others on whom s/he can rely	Controlled by others, less reliable
Labour	Unlimited, no constraint	Hired, few constraints	Family, constraining at seasonal peaks
Prices	Irrelevant	Lower than for RPF for inputs. Higher than RPF for outputs	Higher than for RRF for inputs. Lower than RRF for outputs
Priority for food production	Neutral	Low	High
Access to extension services	Good, but one sided	Good, almost all material designed for this category	Poor access, little relevant material

Source: Chambers and Jiggins (1986), adapted from Chambers and Ghildyal (1985)

17

the limits within which the approach is meant to be applied. One can, however, identify those circumstances and locations which are commonly excluded. These include high potential, irrigated and uniform agricultural areas where relatively better soils and climatic conditions – and the use of agricultural inputs – support high yields. Agricultural experiment stations are frequently located in areas such as these: where station and farmer conditions are similar, direct farmer involvement in the research process may be of secondary importance, as farmers themselves often keep in close touch with the research services. Amongst others, Chambers and Ghildyal (1985) have drawn attention to the similarities between research station conditions and those of 'resource-rich' farmers (Table 2.1). Under these relatively favoured conditions there may be some basis to expect limited benefits from farmer participation in research that goes beyond the initial identification of research opportunities and final field testing.

It is now a well-known story that over the last forty years considerable research emphasis has been placed on the generation of high-yielding crop varieties and management strategies for use in high potential – often irrigated – areas (Lipton, 1989). The fundamental objective was to produce a marketable food surplus to feed burgeoning populations, particularly in urban areas. Underlying this was the philosophy that the use of inputs would overcome environmental differences and that basic packages would be sufficiently productive so that market forces would ensure the development of the necessary input delivery and marketing systems. Thus most commodity-based research programmes took as their starting point increased productivity of land, and promoted a package of improved practices which included high-yielding varieties, fertilizer and improved management. Major indicators of performance were yield and economic return per hectare. The main focus of the research was on irrigated rice, wheat and maize. This approach, and the associated 'green revolution technology', led to dramatic increases in food production in some areas (and a lively and continuing debate around the issues such as sustainability, biodiversity, equity and environmental and social impacts).

It is now also widely accepted that an alternative approach, less dependent on external inputs and able to cope with ecological uncertainty and diversity, is required for poor people farming in low potential areas.[5] Cropping systems in these areas are considered to be more complex and diverse, requiring a 'systems approach' to both analysis and improvement. Individuals and institutions promoting farmer participatory research have consequently aligned themselves closely with those espousing sustainable

---

[5] It has been pointed out that there can be crises in high potential areas which may be vital parts of a country's grain production system. Such areas may also require an alternative approach (D. Gibbon, personal communication).

agriculture on the one hand, and the use of systems approaches on the other (Brown and Wolf, 1985; Altieri and Anderson, 1986; Dover and Talbot, 1987). For example, in some situations an agro-ecological, resource management approach to technology development has been promoted in which foresters, water management specialists and ecologists are added to the research team. Within this framework, the timetable is long term, the focal point is the village or watershed and the client is the whole society. However, some authors have suggested that the resulting increase in the complexity and scale of the research agenda and methodologies dramatically increases the gap between what *needs to be done* and what most research teams *can actually do* (Posner and Gilbert, 1991).

At a technological level, the aim of farmer participatory research is to understand the main characteristics and dynamics of the agro-ecosystem within which the community operates, to identify priority problems and opportunities, and to experiment locally with a variety of technological 'options' based on ideas and experiences derived from indigenous knowledge and formal science. It is important to note that farmer participatory research, because of its focus on poor farmers in diverse, low potential areas, is not in principle concerned – or expected – to generate innovations with potential for wide adoption or applicability although the underlying ideas may well find wider applicability (Fujisaka, 1993).[6]

Agricultural research and farmers

...knowledge generation and utilization are not merely matters of instrumentalities, technical efficiency, or hermeneutics... but involve aspects of control, authority and power that are embedded in social relations (Long and Long, 1992).

At its simplest, farmer participatory research refers to the involvement of farmers in a process of agricultural research. There is, however, no explicit statement or implicit assumption about the nature or level of their involvement. Hence, it is largely practitioners themselves, whether associated with development agencies or research institutions, who are determining these critical parameters. While the examples presented in Chapter 5 will illustrate that there is agreement among a wide variety of institutions on the need for farmer participation in the research process, there are at the same time wide differences in both opinion and practice

---

[6] We suggest that this has major implications for research institutions in terms of the level of financial and human resources than can be justifiably allocated to farmer participatory research, a theme which is taken up again in Chapter 6.

Table 2.2 Characteristics of four modes of farmer participation in agricultural research

	Mode of participation			
	Contract	Consultative	Collaborative	Collegial
Type of relationship	Farmers, land and services are hired or borrowed, e.g., the researcher contracts with the farmer to provide specific types of land	There is a doctor-patient relationship. Resaerchers consult farmers, diagnose their problems and try to find solutions	Researchers and farmers are partners in the research process and continuously collaborate in activities	Researchers actively encourage the informal R & D system in rural areas

Source: Biggs (1989)

over the central issue of how they should participate, for what purpose, at what stage and in what kinds of programmes.

Both the locations and the people designated as clients of participatory research are frequently marginalized within national political life (Amanor, 1990). Consequently, problems of local empowerment and social organization are considered by some to be integral to the discussion of development in general and of farmer participatory research in particular. While the development of technology is one objective of closer researcher–farmer interaction, therefore, farmer participatory research is also viewed as an empowering process whereby those with a legitimate interest in the outcome of research are able to exert some influence on priorities and decisions. Given the diversity of situations, both institutional and programmatic, within which farmer participatory research is being used, approaches to participation and to the whole issue of empowerment vary considerably.

For example Ashby (1992), writing from within an international agricultural research centre and taking a rather restrained view, describes participation as 'the increasing devolution to farmers of the major responsibility for adaptive testing and sharing of accountability for quality control over research among the organizations taking part.' Others argue that the objectives of empowerment and better social organization distinguish farmer participatory research from other client-led research approaches (although it is clearly a matter of opinion as to where one ends and another begins). Biggs's (1989) framework, which describes the relationship between research partners in terms of the extent to which local opinion and practice is given recognition (which we might refer to broadly as empowerment in the sense in which it can be addressed within the confines of farmer participatory research), is now widely used to classify types of participatory research and development activities. The four categories – contractual, consultative, collaborative and collegiate – describe increasing degrees of farmer involvement in decision-making and

20

Table 2.3 Indicators of participation

Stage	Indicator
Information sharing	Beneficiaries receive information about project aims and how it will effect them. Helps facilitate action.
Consultation	People are not only informed but are also consulted on key issues. Beneficiaries may provide feedback to project managers who may use the information to influence project design and implementation.
Decision-making	Beneficiaries involved in decision-making about project design and implementation.
Initiating action	Beneficiaries propose action to initiate themselves.

Note: This is not a hierarchical presentation. The appropriate level of participation depends on the type of project and the socio-economic environment in which it is being implemented.

Source: Paul (1986)

hence increasing levels of equality between the parties involved (Table 2.2). The first three of these categories describe functional participation. The contractual mode implies little interest on the part of the researcher in farmer knowledge or informal research processes. Within the consultative and collaborative modes the researcher recognizes the importance of local information and understanding: farmers tap their knowledge about local conditions and innovations to inform researchers, who are then better placed to do research under farmers' conditions. The last mode of participation, collegiate, puts emphasis on strengthening and providing support to informal research processes by building on existing skills and knowledge, and thus embodies elements of a much broader objective of empowerment.

At a programme level, participation is often characterized in terms of the point or stage at which clients are involved in decision-making, such as problem diagnosis, research design, implementation, monitoring or evaluation. There are also other schema. The World Bank Learning Group, for example, has proposed a schema which combines the quality aspects of Biggs's modes of participation with the stage at which the participation takes place (Paul, 1986). Four levels of participation are described: information sharing, consultation, decision-making and initiating action (Table 2.3).

While reports of farmer participatory research cover activities and programmes being carried out at all these levels, and there is clearly no 'best' mode or level of participation, many practitioners claim to be concerned to operate as closely as possible to the collegiate mode. Thus, as we note in later chapters, programmes report positively on their attempts to move from contractual to collaborative research modes. In addition, some facets of the literature place considerable emphasis on a distinction between farmer participatory research and other research approaches, particularly farming systems research, within which farmers also participate.

The idea of co-operating with farmers is certainly not new. As Biggs (1989) points out in his historical review of agricultural research in Asia and Africa, colonial researchers were not ignorant of the value of farmer co-operation. The current interest in farmer participatory research follows closely on two decades of interest and investment in both appropriate technology and farming systems research. It is somewhat ironic, therefore, that much of the participatory research literature seems to go to extraordinary lengths to distance itself from farming systems research, with which it shares many common elements, including farmer participation, multi-disciplinarity and location specificity (Lightfoot and Noble, 1992). The major critiques of farming systems research are reviewed by Farrington and Martin (1987) who also describe the links between the various models of participatory, on-farm and client-oriented research. Major aspects of the critique of farming systems research are its lack of concern with policy and hence narrow focus on technology (Biggs and Farrington, 1991b), the use of commodity or discipline-based problem analyses and lack of attention to differentiation within rural communities, particularly along lines of wealth and gender (Jiggins, 1984). Perhaps less widely discussed is the focus within farming systems research on the identification and alleviation of constraints, whereas farmer participatory research, at least in principle, begins with an emphasis on flexibility and opportunities and an appreciation of local initiative and enterprise.

The description by Farrington and Martin of the succession of attempts to increase farmer participation in research probably best demonstrates the

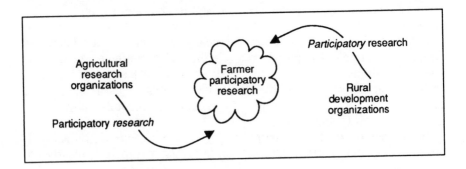

Figure 2.2 *Interpretation of farmer participatory research depends on institutional orientation*

continued dissatisfaction with attempts to incorporate farmers' agendas into agricultural research. The top-down, centre-outward or transfer of technology approach is the most popular whipping boy and therefore provides a common denominator against which most subsequent models are evaluated. Transfer of technology was followed by an emphasis on the modification of the research agenda by feedback (farming systems research and extension), and later by models referred to as 'farmer-back-to-farmer' (Rhoades and Booth, 1982) and 'farmer first and last' (Chambers and Ghildyal, 1985). All of these identified the continuing need to put farmers at the centre of the research process. More recently there has been a call to move 'beyond farmer first' through the addition of a political agenda incorporating basic changes in power relationships and thus addressing the empowerment issue head on (Scoones and Thompson, 1992).

Implementing participatory research

...the question of the empowerment of local people cannot be adequately addressed within the confines of farmer participatory research (Amanor, 1990).

What is farmer participatory research as evidenced by actual field experience? This is essentially the subject of the present study. It should be obvious that the actual choice of the type, level and intensity of farmer participation in agricultural research is determined, in practice, by many factors. Reports from the field suggest that farmers and researchers are working jointly in numerous ways within a range of institutional settings. As noted previously, the principal objective of many of these institutions is the empowerment of local people through the implementation of a general development agenda, to which agricultural research may well be only peripheral. On the other hand, there are agricultural research programmes that are very much concerned with 'technical' issues related to agricultural production or improving processing operations, and that are deeply involved in farmer participatory research. In many cases these institutions are less concerned with the discussion of, or research about, new social organizations. In general, therefore, farmer participatory research is associated with two often distinct traditions, agricultural research on the one hand, and community development on the other. The actual orientation and emphasis of any given project depends, in large part, on the tradition of the implementing organization, with more or less weight being given to either participation or research (Figure 2.2). The activities reviewed during the course of this study originate from both sources.

The literature about farmer participatory research is characterized by a discussion of dualisms: interdisciplinary versus disciplinary, holistic versus reductionist, farming systems versus farmer participatory research. This polarization of the debate, and the dichotomized thinking that it reflects, is itself highly problematic. In general, there is an attempt to break the link between research and positivist science, but in practice this often proves difficult. There is, nevertheless, general agreement on the steps in the research process, and three are mentioned in almost all programmes: the identification of opportunities and constraints, the identification of ideas and options for addressing these opportunities and constraints, and the testing and adaptation of ideas and options.

Decisions about who actually participates in the research process are central to all programmes. While many find it relatively simple to define the ultimate beneficiaries of the research as the rural poor living in marginal locations, it is clear that not everyone can, will wish or possibly should be expected to participate in the research. Who participates ultimately depends on a number of factors including the research objectives, the nature of the participation in the sense of how much time will be involved, the skills required and the interest of potential partners in the subject under investigation. In general there are two extreme positions, on the one hand, the selection of a small number of 'researcher farmers', and on the other, the involvement of the whole community. Regardless of the actual criteria used for selection, since there is almost always an assumption of collective action implicit in the empowerment objective of farmer participatory research, there must be some sense that those who participate are representative of or represent the views of all potential beneficiaries.

Summary

For the most part, the discussion of farmer participatory research is being framed in terms of direct interaction between formal agricultural research systems and the farmers' own informal research, a framework which excludes research implemented by farmers or researchers alone. We, however, include the possibility of farmers and researchers being involved at any or all points along a continuum of levels of participation (Figure 2.3). As we shall see, the activities at the two ends of the continuum vary considerably, but both extremes have clear implications for farmer participatory research. This is particularly true of farmers' own research which is not considered to play a particular role within either what might be termed 'traditional' or farming systems research, but which – at least in principle – is central to farmer participatory research. In all cases, these research activities take place within a political, social, economic and agro-climatic context, and it is suggested by some writers that in certain situations, that context may not support farmer participation in research (Biggs and Farrington, 1991b; Biggs, 1989; Gubbels, 1992a; Bebbington and Thiele, 1993; Pretty and Chambers, 1992). Thus the clear concern of some organizations and authors with policy, institutions and organization referred to earlier. This concern with creating a more enabling context for participatory research has been associated with some projects that have attempted to change the nature of formal research organizations (Merrill-Sands and Kaimowitz, 1990).

3 Associated Themes and Concepts

IN CHAPTER 2 the broad outlines of farmer participatory research were presented. This introduction identified several themes which underlie much of the current interest in farmer participatory research: empowerment, local knowledge, the interface between knowledge systems, rural livelihood systems and sustainable agriculture. These themes form the intellectual context within which the interest in farmer participatory research is situated. As such, these themes are critical to our understanding of farmer participatory research, and they are therefore discussed in the present chapter under six inter-related headings: (i) modernization and technology, (ii) participation and research, (iii) empowerment, (iv) knowledge, (v) low input, sustainable systems and (vi) methods. All six areas are the subject of large and diverse bodies of literature which cannot be reviewed in detail in the present study. Rather, this chapter pinpoints a number of concerns related to these themes which are particularly relevant to an analysis of farmer participatory research. Some of these same concerns are also addressed in subsequent chapters which review recent experiences with the implementation of farmer participatory research.

Modernization and technology

Farmer participatory research and the development agendas associated with it are invariably contrasted with modernization and technocratic approaches to development which featured strongly in the development literature of the 1960s[1]. Moore (1963:89) described modernization as a:

> "total" transformation of a traditional or pre-modern society into the types of technology and associated social organization that characterize the "advanced" economically prosperous, and relatively politically stable nations of the western world.

---

[1] For a historical review of social science analyses see Biggs and Farrington (1991a). For a review of the various approaches which have been used for looking at the food crisis and agrarian change in Africa see Berry (1984).

26

Modernization theories of social change developed out of the colonial experience and evolutionary theories of species development. In this view the modernization process was triggered by contact between two worlds, and the persistence of traditional features was associated with cultural lag. The same period was characterized by a whole literature on socio-cultural constraints (organizational requirements for industrialization, etc.) and writers seeking to explain why one ethnic group appeared to be more ready to change than another (e.g., Ottenberg, 1962; Schneider, 1962). The widespread acceptance of a model of cultural evolution was grounded in the work of Spencer, Darwin and Marx (Richards, 1985). In addition to this cultural model, other evolutionary models have been proposed (e.g., Boserup, 1965), and some continue to carry considerable weight in the discussion of change within agricultural systems (Pingali *et al.*, 1987; McIntire *et al.*, 1992; Tiffen and Mortimore, 1992).

Perhaps one of the weakest aspects of modernization theory is the implied stagnation of 'traditional' society and culture. It is ironic, therefore, that while modernization theory itself has fallen from favour, this view of stagnant traditional societies has proven remarkably persistent. Thus, numerous project documents and country profiles by donor agencies continue to depict an earlier, almost timeless rural scene. This scenario is often fortified with examples of 'recent' commercialization within 'traditional' communities previously producing (so we are told) only for 'subsistence'. Earlier periods of commercialization and change are conveniently forgotten (Caldas, 1992). Rhoades (1987) indicates, however, that this is a limited historical view of change, as modern agriculture is a mere 'afterthought to some 10,000 years of farmer experimentation and technological breakthroughs'.

The concept of rural people as innovators has been explored over a wider canvas than simply technical innovations, particularly in Africa. Polly Hill's studies of migrant Ghanaian cocoa farmers describe the formation of new social groupings specifically for the purpose of acquiring and developing land for cocoa plantations (Hill, 1963), and in later work she explores capitalist ventures amongst fishermen and herders (Hill, 1970). Sara Berry (1975;1985) documents non-agricultural investment by Nigerian cocoa farmers in response to changing opportunities: they invested heavily in education when this became the more beneficial avenue for future advancement. Kerven (1992) examines marketing strategies of pastoral societies in East and West Africa. These groups effectively changed their patterns of grazing and marketing behaviour in response to, among other things, changing government policy. Others including Handwerker (1973) in Liberia and Parkin (1972) in Kenya have also demonstrated the propensity of rural Africans to innovate and adapt in changing circumstances. These studies are part of a larger body of evidence, including work cited by Long and Long (1992) from Costa Rica, Mexico and Zambia, which records the way rural people perceive and cope with change in the course of their daily lives.

However, there are clearly limitations to this argument. The ability of individuals to affect their situation depends on various political, cultural, social, economic and personal factors. Some argue, therefore, that research and information dissemination will achieve little in many countries unless accompanied by changes in the broader political economy. These debates have drawn attention to the issue of equity, differential distribution of resources and gender.

Boserup (1970) effectively rearranged the major lines of discussion and research by hammering home the involvement and contribution of women in all aspects of agricultural production. Since that time, national governments and international research and development agencies have been challenged to incorporate women as active agents in development programmes. Varying levels of effort and success are evident (see Staudt, 1985; Cloud, 1987; Stamp, 1989; Poats, 1991; Ellerston, 1991). While it is now widely recognized that men and women have different roles in rural production systems and consequently have different needs, translating this understanding into practical programmes has been problematic (Mosher, 1989).

The criticisms of a simplistic, 'modern', technocratic approach to agricultural development emerged in the 1960s (e.g., Spicer, 1962), and partly in response, the community development approach emphasized location specificity, grassroots involvement and 'felt needs'. An interest in 'appropriate technology' was already evident by the early 1970s, with a focus on low-cost technology, based on local materials, and simplicity of production methods, operation and maintenance.

The other critique of the technocratic school attacked the view of technology as moving from the centre to the periphery or from the top to the bottom. The discipline of rural sociology as it emerged in the United States, epitomized by the work of Rogers (1962) on the *Theory of Adoption and Diffusion of Innovations*, is a classic example of this tradition. Again, by the early 1970s there was already a move away from these simple, linear models. Thus Cliffe (1973) insists that farmers should be provided with alternatives, which they themselves have helped determine, and among which they can choose. The continuing preoccupation with shifting technology development from the top and centre to the bottom and periphery, and the emphasis on the multiple sources of innovation, must be seen as part of this same movement.

It is the subject of farmer experimentation which links the discussion of development and change with strategies for the development and dissemination of agricultural technology. The work of Richards (1986; 1989) in Sierra Leone has been particularly influential, especially because of his detailed analysis of active experimentation within the agricultural production system. Other similar work (Brammer, 1980; Ghildyal, 1987) reports active farmer involvement in matching rice varieties to environmental conditions.

Biggs (1980) refers specifically to farmers' contribution to the development of crop varieties and genetic diversity, and the history of the movement and incorporation of new crops into existing farming systems provides incontestable evidence worldwide of peoples' willingness and ability to incorporate new ideas and practices without external support. Farmer innovations are not limited to crop varieties. The case of the bamboo tubewell from India (Clay, 1974; Dommen, 1975) is widely referenced because of the apparent phenomenal success of a technology developed by a single farmer: within four years, 33,000 tubewells were reported to have been in use in Bihar State alone.

It has become increasingly clear that technical interventions cannot be seen within a simple evolutionary perspective as they are only one of many possible factors affecting technical and social change:

> it is necessary to be aware of the complex processes by which agricultural resources are mobilized and managed and the changing links between surveyed households and wider spheres of economic and social change (Berry, 1984).

In addition, the recent literature on human agency highlights the fact that intervention processes can rarely be managed to follow a strict implementation plan (Long, 1992). Rather, interventions should be informed by the concept of 'strategic agency', as the way in which people deal with and participate in the constraining and enabling elements and try to enrol each other in their various endeavours (Long and Long, 1992). Thus, similar structural circumstances or interventions can produce a highly diverse pattern of responses and outcomes, as a result of a complicated mix of intended and unintended consequences of human action. Indeed, there are many examples of unintended meanings and outcomes of technology development and dissemination.[2]

Participation and research

It is widely accepted that the agriculture technology system can be divided into sub-systems comprised of actors carrying out specific

---

[2] Recent studies of the impact of maize research in Africa, for example, indicate that in some situations farmers used yield increasing technology to decrease the area of maize cultivated. Thus, while adoption of the innovations resulted in neither increased cultivated area or increased production (the official objectives), farmers made valuable resources available for other activities (Gilbert et al., 1993).

functions. According to this schema, basic research develops new knowledge, strategic research solves specific problems, applied research develops new technologies based on knowledge generated from basic and strategic research and adaptive research effects changes in the technologies to adapt them to specific regions and producer groups (Kaimowitz et al., 1990). The technology transfer sub-system facilitates the adoption of technologies by users. All aspects of the agriculture technology system involve farmers to a greater or lesser extent.

The move to farming systems research was, in part, a response to the early Green Revolution experience. Attention began to shift from returns to land towards an analysis of the farm family and its aspirations and resources (Norman, 1980). A better understanding of local farming systems came to be considered essential for the successful development of new technology. At the same time the growing concern with the impact of poverty and population growth on the environment focused attention on the idea of sustainable agriculture.

While farming systems research is still very much alive, in recent years there has been a distinct dampening of interest among some major donors even though there is a legitimate argument that it is only now that the full impact of farming systems research can be seen. This has been largely in response to critics who have questioned its results and impacts, and in line with broader changes in emphasis among donors (e.g., to natural resource management, sustainable agriculture and policy issues). Analyses of the impact of farming systems research and extension extend from tepid (Merrill-Sands and Collion, 1992) to positive (Tripp, 1991) in terms of both the production and adoption of technologies.

As previously noted, a major critique levelled at farming systems research by some proponents of farmer participatory research relates to its lack of any inherent political orientation.[3] Thus, while farming systems research was intentionally popularized as 'participatory research' in the sense that research themes were identified through farm-based diagnostic exercises, and there was some joint testing of technologies, the analysis continued to be made by and within the formal research system. The critique maintains that researchers essentially used the participatory process to validate their own perspectives or actions, and this process has been described as both extractive and disempowering (Chambers, 1992).

The push by donors to establish and institutionalize farming systems

---

[3] It must be noted that the early frameworks presented by Gilbert et al. (1980) and CIMMYT (1988) for the analysis of farming systems included policies and institutions as important external or exogenous factors. Yet, while a number of agricultural research institutions expanded work to include activities outside crop production and intra- and inter-household dynamics, broader policy and political issues were never widely addressed (Baker, 1992; Biggs and Farrington, 1991b).

research teams and units coincided with a series of other events and measures that also had important implications for the interaction of farmers with formal agricultural research. In the late 1980s the donors attempted to promote radical restructuring of agricultural research institutions. The establishment of ISNAR in 1980 was a landmark in this respect: the explicit focus of its mandate on national agricultural research systems suggests a perception (at least within the Consultative Group for International Agricultural Research [CGIAR]) that the problems of the 'agricultural technology system' were primarily to be found within these institutions. ISNAR initiated a series of studies looking at co-ordination and collaboration within research systems and means to improve linkages with extension. More recent institutional reforms funded largely by the World Bank have had a similar focus. These are, for example, attempting to foster the decentralization of decision-making within research systems by setting up regional research steering committees comprised of government officials, researchers and farmers (e.g., in Bangladesh, The Gambia, Malawi and Kenya). One recent observation of the effect of these efforts is that they have resulted in more client-led researchers but not to more client-led research organizations (Merrill-Sands and Collion, 1992). In response, it must be pointed out that it is still early days, and somewhat unrealistic to expect any radical institutional change to have occurred.

In contrast with the pressure on national research systems to increase the level of local involvement, Fujisaka (1992) suggests that the level of farmer participation in the work of the institutes funded through the CGIAR is actually decreasing. While the activities of these institutions vary considerably, and indeed the work of one features prominently among the examples of farmer participatory research discussed in Chapter 4, they are increasingly being used for 'strategic' and 'basic' research, which are generally regarded as having little if any scope for farmer participation.

At the same time, NGOs are now seen as appropriate partners for the national research systems (see ODI's recent publications on this subject). The emphasis on the comparative advantages of NGOs in adaptive research and the 'natural' links between NGOs and farmer participatory research reflects a general frustration with the formal, governmental, research and extension institutions. The field orientation of most NGOs is seen to place them in an ideal position to carry out the more local, adaptive and participatory functions of the agricultural technology system.[4] These considerations have coalesced into what we argue is a

---

[4] However, Lehmann (1990) has commented generally that unless NGOs become more skilful and seek policy change ('instead of investing in a hope for more direct and participatory democracy'), they will not be effective.

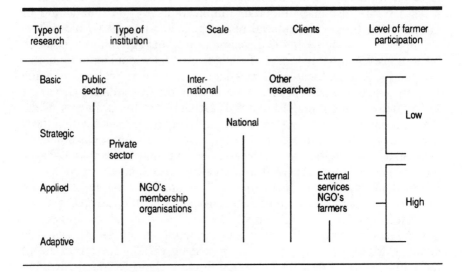

Type of research	Type of institution	Scale	Clients	Level of farmer participation
Basic	Public sector	Inter-national	Other researchers	Low
Strategic	Private sector	National		
Applied	NGO's membership organisations		External services NGO's farmers	High
Adaptive				

Figure 3.1 *Participation and the agricultural technology system: a widely held view*

simplistic and highly compartmentalized view of the research components of the agricultural technology system (Figure 3.1).

Many practitioners would agree that whether framed in terms of farming systems research or farmer participatory research, the basic objectives and principles of farmer participation in agricultural research remain the same: it is really only the emphasis that has changed. For example, over the last ten years there has been considerable movement of professionals between the fields of farming systems research, farmer participatory research and sustainable agriculture, and the same authors appear in each set of literature. There are those who struggle to push farming systems research further into the realms of systems analysis and farmer participation (Lightfoot and Noble, 1992; Fujisaka, 1993), others who seek to draw clear distinctions between the approaches (Chambers and Ghildyal, 1985; Chambers and Jiggins, 1986; Chambers, 1992; Scoones and Thompson, 1992) and still others who make distinctions but place both approaches within a single framework of agricultural research (Jiggins, 1992).

The detailed reviews presented in later chapters will show clearly that on-going farmer participatory research has much in common with farming systems research, and individuals and institutions involved in farmer participatory research are part of the larger body of people and institutions seeking to increase the levels of farmer participation in agricultural research.[5] We suggest that attempts to understand farmer participatory research independent of farming systems research will thus yield little of value. Similarly, the non-historical perspective of those who argue that farmer participatory research is an entirely new paradigm, with (or in need of) unique bodies of theory and practice, will only act to marginalize whatever potential value the approach might have.

Empowerment

There is a large body of literature emphasizing the exploitation of the peasantry by the state or by the new agrarian bourgeoisie which is integrated in the discussion of participation and empowerment vis-à-vis farmer participatory research (see for example, Nuijten, 1992 and Bebbington and Thiele, 1993). These political economy analyses are especially common (and compelling) in the context of Latin America, and must be seen in relation to the work of Freire (1972), the Brazilian educationalist who advocated a direct approach to political empowerment through raising consciousness (using popular education) and organization. Cromwell and Wiggins (1993), in a discussion of empowerment which is informed by the ideas of Freire, refer to 'the creation of an environment of enquiry in which people question and resist the structural reasons for their poverty, through learning and action.'

The focus of the arguments in this literature is to question whether any research activity can lead to empowerment of the poor (and to resistance to government and more powerful others). The argument is that the adoption of innovations cannot take place unless the capacity of the receivers is properly developed (Cromwell and Wiggins, 1993). However, as noted by Long (1992), despite the current discourse that stresses listening, the value of local knowledge, etc., it is difficult to escape the 'notion of powerful outsiders helping powerless insiders.'

There are other senses in which farmer participation in formal research has been seen as empowering. Bunch (1982) writes that: 'the main goal of development projects should be to train and motivate farmers to continue the process of innovation and technological adaptation', and Brown (1991) refers to the 'demystifying' of certain activities by the handing over of skills and knowledge. Carroll (1992) has argued that the 'heart' of participation is the capacity of clients to 'create new systems and mechanisms to accomplish their goals' (and in the context of this study the new systems and mechanisms relate to agriculture). PROSHIKA

---

[5] Along these same lines, Jiggins (1992), in her paper for the 12th annual meeting of The Association for Farming Systems Research/Extension, suggested that farming systems research might be viewed as a bridge between conventional research ('formal science') and the 'emerging body of experience with participatory technology development' (farmer participatory research).

(a non-governmental organization in Bangladesh) points to the importance of economic activities for making non-economic activities (such as consciouness raising) effective.

At one level there is obvious truth in Amanor's (1990) observation that the question of empowerment of local people cannot be adequately addressed within the confines of farmer participatory research. Nevertheless, a research approach which in theory starts with an analysis by local people, and clearly places greater emphasis on the farmers' own (as against the researchers') capacity to solve problems or seize opportunities, must be considered as potentially empowering. Certainly the strategies of adult education and community organization that are sometimes associated with farmer participatory research should 'elevate the claim-making capacity of the people, to "empower" them...so that they can effectively press their demands...and...pull down services to themselves' (Villareal, 1992). We need to be very clear, however, that farmer participatory research, in the sense of a research approach, a project or a series of specific activities designed to address agricultural or agriculturally-related issues, can never in itself fully address the 'wider conscientizing political aspects of empowerment'.

However, if one accepts that the outcomes of farmer participatory research are not simply the production of particular technologies (but also the increased ability of those clients with a legitimate interest in the outcomes of research to exert some influence on priorities and decisions), and that not all participation is necessarily empowering (Whyte, 1991), then the contractual level of participation within Biggs's framework is simply not enough. At the same time, the process of changing the power relations between researchers and farmers can be initiated in a variety of ways. Farmer participatory research will not be sufficient in that, for the most part, it takes place in the field, at the level of farm families and communities and between individual researchers and groups of farmers. Merrill-Sands and Collion (1992), Biggs (1989) and Ashby (1992) have all recently noted this same issue, and institutional mechanisms for resolving it have been the concern of some donors for a number of years.

Knowledge systems

Much of the discussion about empowerment and power relations is directly related to the interest in knowledge systems, and in particular to the relationship between 'indigenous technical knowledge' and 'scientific' knowledge. This discussion is also characterized by a series of dichotomies, with knowledge being described as either 'insider' or 'outsider', 'formal' or 'informal,' 'local' or 'scientific'. A comprehensive definition is provided by van der Bliek and van Veldhuizen (1993), with indigenous knowledge referring to:

ideas, experiences, practices, information that has been generated locally, or is generated elsewhere but has been transformed by local people and incorporated in the local way of life. Indigenous knowledge incorporates local technologies but also cultural, social and economic aspects.

This definition incorporates the idea that indigenous knowledge is shared and accumulated in social groups (see Brokensha *et al.*, 1980 and Richards, 1985). With reference to community environmental knowledge, Richards (1978) argues that it should be looked at as a system: it is an interconnected, multidimensional matrix of data, symbols and values rather than a miscellaneous collection of factual items. The literature makes reference to the fact that ethno-science has highlighted many examples of folk knowledge of nature and in some of this work there is the search for human universals. There are detailed studies of folk systematics, with emphasis on classification, nomenclature and identification (Berlin, 1973). Howes and Chambers (1979) have argued that the strongest contribution of indigenous knowledge to agricultural research is just such systems of classification of the biophysical environment.

Indigenous or local knowledge is frequently contrasted with outsider knowledge: 'the mode of indigenous technical knowledge is "concrete" and it relies almost exclusively on intuition and on evidence directly available to the senses. As a system of explanation and prediction and in terms of speed of knowledge accumulation, it is likely to be inferior to formal science' (Howes and Chambers, 1979). Similarly, '...local knowledge is constrained since it is passed on orally or by direct experience and held in the heads of practitioners' (Swift, 1979). Indigenous and outsider knowledge are even viewed in a number of instances as being in conflict (Salas, 1992; Uquillas, 1992) and hence no synthesis between them is likely: they will either be kept separate or local knowledge will be ignored (Howes and Chambers, 1979). Others are less concerned about the erosion of local knowledge than about the undermining of processes of indigenous adaptations when people are not given relevant information underpinning new production techniques (Bell, 1979). These images of separateness and conflict have brought some writers to suggest that local and non-local knowledge systems are essentially incompatible (which would clearly undermine the rationale for participatory research).

More recently, however, some of the same authors have begun to emphasize the similarities rather than the differences. Thus Chambers (1992) remarked that there is much overlap between 'popular' and scientific knowledge: 'both appear to understand topics like the growth stages of plants and the benefits of irrigation'. Likewise, Fairhead (1993)

35

reporting on field studies in Guinea observed that farmers' knowledge is more empirical and dynamic than he had imagined. In fact, these views correspond with those expressed earlier by Richards (1978), who observed that '...so-called "traditional" societies have well developed methods of collecting and acting upon empirical knowledge which compare with the methods of organized science' (p.28). There have certainly been some calls for caution in the midst of the general enthusiasm over the value of local knowledge (Bentley, 1991). Nevertheless, a recognition of the value of local knowledge lies at the heart of the interest in farmer participatory research.

Unfortunately there appears to have been less attention given to the question of advantages to farmers of researcher knowledge (and hence the value to farmers of increased interaction with formal research). Clearly researchers potentially have access to a wider body of knowledge than do farmers and perhaps this is their greatest advantage. They also examine relationships in a different way, which could be advantageous although it has not yet been demonstrated that these methods are any better for answering site-specific questions than the farmers' own. Richards (1978) emphasizes the potential value of formal research in protecting local knowledge from 'erosion' (by moving knowledge around) and in supplementing endogenous systems by identifying critical weakness. Biggs and Clay (1980) provide a long list of limitations of informal research (and thereby the advantages of formal research): it is restricted to using local gene pools and new material introduced by random transfer; vulnerable to environmental change or unforseen consequences of technological transfer; genetic possibilities in the case of self-pollinating crops requiring systematic breeding techniques, not explored; not forward looking and therefore unable to anticipate opportunities and the risks of changing factor endowments and environments, or to explore possibilities where a costly and lengthy process of research is required.

The debate concerning the nature, structure and value of indigenous or local knowledge is multifaceted, complex and verbose. However, some aspects of this debate are more important for our analysis of farmer participatory research than others. The differentiated nature of local knowledge is widely discussed and is used by some to question the value of 'ethno-scientific models', which 'assume that cultural understandings provide the ground rules for social life that remain the same for members of the same epistemic community' (Arce and Long, 1992). Richards (1978) cites various levels of differentiation: local ecology and human geography, age, sex and class affiliation. Attention has been drawn in particular to the difference between men's and women's knowledge, and while this is frequently associated with sex-role differences, we are also warned not to assume that knowledge is limited to areas within which people have roles to play (Fairhead, 1992). Others have been concerned to distinguish between different kinds of knowledge, such as transmitted and learned through experience (Rhoades and Bebbington, 1991), and between practices that are fortuitous side consequences and those that are informed by knowledge (Fairhead, 1993).

However, farmer participatory research is as much about creating and managing a specific interface between local and outsider knowledge as it is about indigenous technical knowledge *per se*.[6] A basic premise underlying the move toward farmer participatory research is that local knowledge has often been ignored and at times actively denigrated, and as such it has been unable to withstand the onslaught of outsider knowledge. Thus, even accepting their proposition that knowledge systems do not come together as equals (Richards, 1989a; Zadek, 1993), the challenge to practitioners of farmer participatory research is to create a situation within which a more equitable sharing of information is possible (one which does not assume that 'scientifically' generated knowledge is of greater value than local knowledge). This is, however, a formidable challenge: as Zadek has emphasized (1993), 'because of the social barriers between peasant farmers and technicians, farmers will not easily disagree with researchers' (p.115) and in general, research institutions regard their knowledge as superior.

There is another body of research that highlights the fact that all information and knowledge is transformed during the process of communication, and that local knowledge is not totally powerless in the face of outsider knowledge. Local people have the capacity to absorb and rework external knowledge and information in the light of their own experience and understanding (e.g., various articles in Long and Long, 1992). Specifically, Arce and Long (1992:214) indicate that:

The production and transformation of knowledge resides in the processes by which social actors interact, negotiate and accommodate to each other's life-worlds, leading to the reinforcement or transformation of existing types of knowledge or to the emergence of new forms.

While much of the farmer participatory research literature appears to reject this more fluid and dynamic view, emphasis at the technical level is placed on *adaptation* rather than adoption or the use of outside knowledge to create whole new production systems. As Long and

---

[6] This is not to say that local cosmologies are necessarily irrelevant to effective agricultural research and extension programmes. As is highlighted in later chapters, the assembly of information about local situations (either for wider dissemination or as a basis for experimentation under controlled conditions), is a component of a number of farmer participatory research programmes.

Villareal (1992:21) have pointed out, adoption and diffusion theory have given way to communications and systems theory: the guiding notions are discontinuity and transformation as opposed to the transfer of meaning. These discussions of communication go far beyond the debate over linkage mechanisms between research, extension and farmers, which spurred the on-farm research movement and which continue to be the focus of some considerable attention.

For the purposes of an analysis of farmer participatory research it is important to distinguish between local knowledge in the sense discussed above and innovative, experimental behaviour in the realm of farming, food processing, etc. While in many situations farmer participatory research is portrayed as researchers and farmers matching their knowledge about trees, plants and soil fertility, there is also the element of handing over of skills and the direct use of farmers' existing experimental skills. The question of differentiated skills is especially relevant to this point since there is an implicit understanding that a collegiate relationship between farmers and researchers develops from a base of compatible research skills (Biggs's notion of 'research-minded farmers'). It would seem unlikely that such an orientation and accompanying research skills would be evenly distributed within communities or populations.

We have indicated that the empowerment theme which underlies much current farmer participatory research has led practitioners to implement participation through groups and whole communities and to direct attention towards particularly disadvantaged groups (women and the poor). However, the differentiation of local knowledge, innovative behaviour and research-mindedness point to a potential conflict between the technology development and testing objective of farmer participatory research and the concern with empowerment more generally.

Low external input, sustainable systems

The development of low external input, sustainable agriculture systems is regarded by many as central to the future of resource-poor farmers in marginal areas (Woodhouse, 1992).[7] 'Traditional' production systems are seen as having much in common with a new generation of low input, sustainable systems, and the logic of participatory research is imposing. This was certainly not the case with farming systems research although there was a growing understanding that technologies such as high-yielding varieties, chemical fertilizers and pesticides were not the solution for many small, low resource producers.

---

[7] At the same time there are those who argue that the nutrient mining of soils is on such a vast scale especially in Sub-Saharan Africa, that low input systems cannot address the problem (B. Pound, personal communication; van Keulen and Breman, 1990).

The technical objectives of low-input, sustainable systems are seen in terms of optimum use of locally available resources (use of external inputs only to complement deficient elements in the ecosystem); maximum recycling of the external inputs; and a stable or increasing level of production. In addition, goals for sustainable agriculture invariably seek to maintain or increase biological and economic productivity, enhance efficiency of inputs used, increase stability of production, increase resilience to environmental changes, minimize adverse environmental impacts, and ensure social compatibility (Lightfoot and Noble, 1992). It is suggested that farmer participatory research can be used to achieve these goals through the development of specific farm practices for each ecological and socio-economic context, as well as developing whole new farm systems with these same characteristics (*ibid*).

As with most other aspects of the literature on farmer participatory research, there is a wider debate surrounding the concept of sustainability. Thus, while the core of the agronomic sustainability argument is that increased biological diversity and internal integration permits farming with fewer chemical inputs and less environmental hazard (Parr *et al.*, 1983; Altieri, 1984; Harwood, 1984), the discussion of sustainable land-use systems also has its political aspects.

The discussion of sustainability and alternative land-use systems also suffers badly from the tendency to dichotomize: Green Revolution techniques for resource wealthy farmers with irrigated land versus low-input systems for poor farmers living in marginal areas. Similarly the debate over local or exotic varieties, composites or hybrids, is well rehearsed. Yet, while it can be demonstrated that problems are created by the loss of local varieties, it is also well documented that the dynamic between local and introduced crop varieties is not necessarily in conflict. New, short-cycle varieties can outperform local, long-cycle varieties in poor years, and many small farmers in Africa are keenly interested in hybrids (Gilbert *et al.*, 1993). Thus, a number of writers have emphasized the need for research and extension to focus on the provision of options and choices rather than single recommendations (Gibbon, 1981; Miles, 1982[8]; Sumberg and Okali, 1988; Chambers, 1989; Versteeg and Koudokpon, 1993; Heinrich, 1993; Okali *et al.*, 1994).

Similarly a number of innovative development activities have demonstrated that with a more flexible, less polarized approach, the production process itself can be broken into various parts to the benefit of different groups. Thus, improved vegetable and sugarcane seedlings for

---

[8] Miles points out that basic to the whole purpose of the appropriate technology philosophy and approach is that there should be a range of technologies available so that people can choose the one which is most appropriate to their particular circumstances and needs.

commercial vegetable producers are produced for sale by landless people in Bangladesh (E. Gilbert, personal communication), while in other situations landless people provide irrigation water to support an intensive rice production system (Wood and Palmer-Jones, 1990).

Finally, it should be remembered that the assertion of the irrelevance of the Green Revolution approach for marginal areas and resource poor farmers, that is made throughout much of the farmer participatory research literature, is not, in fact, reflective of a clear record of failure. As was noted in Chapter 2, these areas have not, in general, been at the centre of attention of agricultural researchers and research institutions.

This discussion of the applicability or appropriateness of one or another type of technology vis-à-vis a particular group of participants approaches the much broader subject of livelihood systems. Farming systems research was critiqued for its limited and narrow focus on agriculture at the expense of other elements of the livelihood system. However, if agricultural research and technology development is viewed within this wider context, the question of sustainability becomes even more complex. Thus, while the arguments about the poor and disenfranchised are compelling, we are aware that these people, along with everyone else, are constantly seeking new strategies for meeting their needs. In the case of the Andes, the Sahelian zone of Africa and tribal areas in Asia, strategies frequently involve seasonal or permanent outmigration of one or more family members. These strategies have major implications for local interest in, and alternatives for, research aimed at the long-term sustainability of the agricultural production system. Some authors have highlighted the fact that system sustainability is enhanced through diversifying enterprises over time and space (Altieri, 1987), but the reality of some real-life diversification strategies flies in the face of the more simplistic and idealistic discussions of sustainability and sustainable agricultural production systems. Well-established patterns of seasonal migration from the West African Sahel to coastal countries, for example, cast considerable doubt on the viability and sustainability of soil conservation interventions that demand heavy investment of labour during the dry season (Painter *et al.*, 1993).

Methodology

...an appropriate research methodology that can facilitate the analysis of social action and interpretation...should not be reduced to methods and techniques of data collection and classification (Long, 1992:268).

The discussion of methods within the farmer participatory research literature can be broken into three parts: the first revolves around a familiar theme within the social sciences, the distinction between qualitative and quantitative techniques and approaches and includes the popularization of participatory techniques and tools, specifically PRA. The second touches more directly on the issue of how to engage in a participatory process and is concerned with enhancing self-awareness and analytical skills on the part of clients and attitude changes on the part of researchers. The third centres on modes of experimentation and distinguishes itself from similar discussions within farming systems research by its emphasis on client participation and control. All three parts of the discussion are interrelated. Thus, issues of quantification feature prominently in the literature on on-farm experimentation and the value of PRA tools is acknowledged as being contingent upon the strength of the participatory process itself. It is also acknowledged that PRA tools are to be used jointly with other research techniques which may be more quantitative in nature.

Underpinning much of the literature on methods for farmer participatory research is a distinction between quantitative and qualitative approaches in applied science. The debate on methods is often reduced to a dichotomy between quantitative versus qualitative studies and techniques, and statistical versus non-statistical approaches. The objective of these discussions is to break the link between what is understood as 'research' and 'positivist science', and they argue for a rejection of any assumption of the neutrality of the scientific method. Some of the more extreme positions were presented at the workshop on 'Qualitative versus Quantitative Approaches in Applied Research and Rural Development' held at Sokoine University in Tanzania (Hoeper, 1990). Hoeper himself argues forcefully that qualitative research (case study material) aims to describe and understand more limited and local realms and is concerned with understanding the perspective of 'the Other', whereas traditional quantitative research techniques are 'sterile,' 'elitist' and 'empirical'. In this discussion qualitative techniques are equated with understanding and respect for others and are clearly viewed as more empowering (of clients).

This critique of quantitative studies and techniques is certainly not new:

The application of maths to sociology does not ensure rigor or proof any more than the use of insight guarantees the significance of the research. The fundamental questions to ask about all research techniques are those dealing with precision, reliability and relevance of data and their analyses (Goode and Hatt, 1952).

However, as Farrington and Bebbington (1993) warn, it is necessary to avoid confusing poor research with the methods and approaches themselves: a reductionist research method does not necessarily lead to a top-down development approach.

Part of the emphasis on qualitative methodological approaches in relation to farmer participatory research is associated with a broader debate about action-oriented research (see for example Scoones and Thompson, 1992). Following Long and Long (1992), action-oriented research can be defined as a theoretical and methodological approach to the understanding of social processes. Its guiding analytical concepts are human agency and the social actor; the notion of multiple realities and arenas of struggle; and the idea of interface, relating discontinuities of interests, negotiation, values, knowledge and power. Long and Long have argued that the actor perspective helps one appreciate the need for a more systematic and sensitive methodology for reaching the 'voices of the people' that include the ongoing transformation and interpretation of local and external models and experience. They therefore emphasize the use of case studies, situational analysis, life histories, social network analysis and the analysis of interface situations.

The shift from agricultural researchers basing their conclusions on studies of the natural world, and to some varying degree the social world, to an incorporation of local peoples' own views of the natural world, has been accompanied by a significant change in research methods. Pretty and Chambers (1992) list 30 participatory approaches and methods 'of the 1980s–1990s'. Among these, PRA tools are probably the most widely used in farmer participatory research. Participatory Rural Appraisal techniques and tools are viewed as the antithesis of quantitative methods and associated directly with participative modes of interaction.[9] They are now used in the context of agricultural research to facilitate what has been described as a 'process of conscious and creative interaction between local communities and outside facilitators' (van der Bliek and van Veldhuizen, 1993). The image is of a joint, collaborative analysis based on locally generated, qualitative information. Thus, the shift in emphasis is seen as reducing the use of methods (usually regarded as quantitative) to 'extract' information from 'insiders' (usually individuals) for analysis by 'outsiders'. There is a whole range of methods or tools associated with PRA-type activities, from those aimed at creating better group dynamics to interviewing, mapping and visual analyses (Cornwall et al., 1992). While the emphasis in much of the PRA literature is on the use of these techniques for problem identification (diagnosis) and prioritization, some have also been used for evaluation and programme monitoring purposes.

---

[9] PRA tools are also widely regarded as ideal for fostering exchange between research disciplines, and thus for systems research, which has become closely associated with farmer participatory research.

More recently, Chambers (1992) has attempted to draw a distinction between techniques and tools which are more 'verbal' or 'observational' and others which are 'visual'. He proceedes to link the verbal and observational tools with farmer participatory research and visual tools with participatory rural appraisal and, while he argues that 'FPR (farmer participatory research) and PRA are complementary and overlapping sources of experiences', the terms he uses suggest something quite different. Thus, he argues that the 'poorer, weaker and women are marginalized rather than empowered' through the use of verbal and observational tools. Verbal tools, in his analysis, are associated with appropriation by outsiders. On the other hand, visual techniques are described as 'creative', 'facilitating' and 'empowering' (Table 3.1). It is difficult to move very far with this kind of comparison as it assumes that PRA and farmer participatory research have the same objectives (which, at any level other than a very general statement about empowerment, is obviously not the case), and that PRA and farmer participatory research are clearly bounded and do not intersect.

The discussion of techniques and tools has been heavily focused on the farmers rather than the researchers:

> Open-ended evaluation stimulates the farmer to think. It can be used to help the farmer marshall thoughts in a sequence, to recall past evaluation(s) and to get into the swing of thinking critically about technology (Quiros *et al.*, 1991).

At the same time, a number of publications, particularly from ISNAR, have emphasized the need for a change in the behaviour of researchers (and extension staff) in order to arrive at any substantial shift in levels of participation by farmers (see Ewell, 1989 for example). Again this concern forms part of the larger debate about the involvement of researchers in client-oriented on-farm research as a whole, and relates to the wider issue of the role of institutions in determining the direction and success of new research approaches (Biggs and Farrington, 1990). Once 'on-farm', there is a clearer appreciation of the inherent value of new approaches for facilitating a different mode of interaction between researchers and clients. Richards (1978), in his discussion of traditional story-telling and traditional games noted that the use of these enabled the 'interviewers' to efface themselves and their internal logic, and to hand over the initiative to the respondent. Referring to Kelly's (1955) discussion of the 'repertory grid technique', Richards emphasizes its 'self analytic and therapeutic intentions'. Robert Chambers (1992) has placed considerable emphasis on these issues in relation to PRA tools and the investment by institutions such as non-governmental organizations and 'enlightened individuals in government organizations' in changing

Table 3.1 An attempt to contrast farmer participatory research with PRA

	Farmer participatory research	Participatory rural appraisal
Scope	Agriculture only	Natural resources, health community planning, agriculture, poverty programmes etc
Main activities	On-farm research and trials	Appraisal and diagnosis
Mode of interaction	More verbal	More visual
Analysis often through	Dialogue	Diagramming
Assessments often through	Absouuloute measurements	Relative comparisons

Source: Chambers (1992)

attitudes, behaviour and facilitation skills of professionals.

Methods, such as DELTA, GRAAP and Training for Transformation, which are associated with enhanced self-awareness and analytical skills of the client communities, are more likely to be identified with more broadly conceived empowerment programmes than with farmer participatory research programmes. They were not, therefore, considered in detail in this study.[10] As was indicated above, PRA tools have been described as having much in common with some of these, including through their use, transferring the responsibility for 'the shaping of local lives, communities and the environment to client communities themselves' (see Chambers, 1992).

The question of methods for participative field trials, tests or experiments is constantly raised at the operational level within farmer participatory research programmes and is discussed in detail at various points in this text. While participation, empowerment and the enhancement of local knowledge and skills are implicit in much of this discussion, there is another more explicit and dominant theme concerning how to do trials with farmers and at the same time maintain scientific integrity, by controlling variability for example. Again, this is not a new discussion: it was a concern of farming systems research, although the more recent discussion of farmer involvement in trial design has moved

---

[10] See Hope and Timmel (1991) and Cornwall et al., (1992) for a listing of these and similar approaches.

Table 3.2 Classification of on-farm trials used within farming systems research

Action	Trial type			
	1	2	3	4
Trial design	Researcher	Researcher	Farmer	Farmer
Trial management	Researcher	Farmer	Researcher	Farmer

far beyond the farming systems research framework of researcher (or farmer) designed and researcher (or farmer) managed trials (Table 3.2). It is interesting to note, that while the value of PRA techniques and tools is almost always presented in terms of qualitative versus quantitative methods, trials are not. In general, trials are viewed as positive and a focal point for real participation and exchange, and the scientific method and formal analysis are seen, and taught, as locally empowering. There are now many manuals which deal specifically with the many types of participative experimentation (Steiner, 1987, 1990; Waters-Bayer, 1989; Ashby, 1990; WRI, 1990; Lightfoot *et al.*, 1990a and 1990b; de Zeeuw and van Veldhuizen, 1992).

Conclusion

In this chapter we have explored some of the key elements which have helped foster and give shape to the current interest in farmer participatory research. The debates around these elements take place at a number of levels, from questions of appropriate designs for field trials to the nature of knowledge systems and the political economy of agrarian change. At all levels, as these debates get nearer to the point of implementation of farmer participatory research, they seem to become increasingly simplistic and dualistic, and their value in informing practical processes is therefore severely limited.

The notion of empowerment is present in all discussions relating to participation, knowledge, agro-ecological systems and even methods and approaches to farmer participatory research. The discussion largely relates to farmers, rather than to researchers and technicians, and the empowerment of farmers is promoted by many as the principle output of farmer participatory research. This is particularly true where farmer participatory research takes place as part of a more general development agenda. Researchers are rarely specifically mentioned in the debates, only science, the scientific approach and government. Rather, it is often assumed that researchers are the same as the government, and not only represent the powerful interests of government, but are themselves powerful. Much recent theory does not allow for more than these two opposing blocs – the powerful state and oppressed peasants – and the commitment of civil society, and non-governmental organizations more specifically, to work between them.

At the same time, there is a large body of literature from which many of the principles of farmer participation have emerged, which illustrates the inherent capacity of rural people to innovate, and hence their ability to exercise some control over their condition. This understanding is related to another important thread in the current discourse which stresses the need for a dynamic analysis of the way in which people, both farmers and representatives of the state (or any other agency), 'struggle, negotiate and compromise' during the process of change (Villareal, 1992). From this point of view, peasants are not passive victims of the state: rather, 'Intervention is constantly being modified by the negotiations and strategies that emerge between the various parties involved' (p.264).

4 Farmer Participatory Research in Practice

HAVING EXPLORED THE theoretical basis for farmer participatory research, Chapters 4 and 5 investigate its scope and nature through an analysis of how it is actually being implemented. Chapter 4 presents examples of approaches being taken by a variety of implementing agencies. Material is drawn from published sources, in addition to information from project files, interviews with practitioners and replies to a mailing sent to all members of ODI's Agricultural Administration (Research and Extension) Network.

Our main interest is to highlight any new understanding of farmer participatory research which has emerged from recent experience gained in the field. As noted in previous chapters, it must be remembered that the broader topic – what has come to be referred to as 'on-farm client-oriented research'[1] – has now been discussed and practised over a period of at least two decades and there have already been a number of in-depth reviews of this experience. The examples do not, however, cover the complete range of participative agricultural research initiatives. Rather, they were selected to illustrate different perspectives vis-à-vis a number of the areas and issues relating directly to farmer participatory research. However, some programmes which have been ongoing for a number of years (particularly some of the national, regional and international agricultural research programmes) are included where their experience has led to new understandings, or changes in approach, which are critical for a broader analysis of farmer participatory research.

A number of key implementation issues are identified in the chapter, including the relationship between theory and practice, and these are at the centre of the analysis presented in Chapters 5 and 6.

A framework

Farmer participatory research is being implemented by a wide variety of

---

[1] Merrill-Sands in Ewell (1989) defines on-farm, client-oriented research (OFCOR) as research designed to meet the needs of specific clients, most commonly resource-poor farmers. 'It involves a client-oriented philosophy, a specific research approach and methods, and a series of operational activities carried out at the farm level...Farmers are directly involved at various stages in the process.'

organizations including national, regional and international research and training institutions, and membership, non-governmental and government organizations involved in development more generally. Each of these organizations has different ideological, institutional and operational orientations and objectives, which give more or less priority to research in general, and agricultural research more specifically. In addition, among these organizations there is a very broad range of training, experience and competence in the conception and implementation of both 'participatory' and 'research' activities. Consequently, there are widely divergent views of how farmer participatory research should be implemented and these views are reflected in on-going field activities.

Two basic approaches have been used in previous reviews of farmer participatory research. The first has been to define the steps in the process of technology development. Thus, Farrington and Martin (1987) structured their review around the different steps inherent in research and problem solving, under the headings of: (i) defining researchable problems, (ii) conducting and evaluating research and (iii) dissemination.

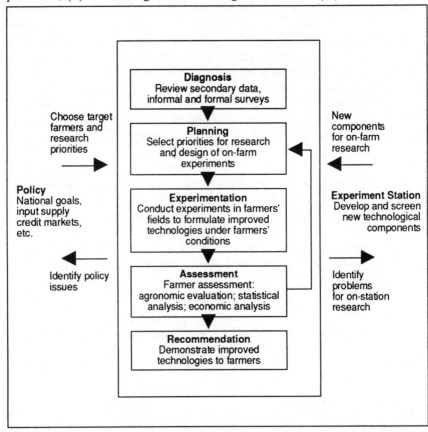

Figure 4.1 *The CIMMYT model of on-farm research* Source: CIMMYT (1988)

Table 4.1 Stages in participatory technology development

	Phase				
	1 How to start	2 Find things to try out	3 Try out new activities	4 Sharing results	5 Sustaining the process
Objectives	Engage in a relationship with the farmers	Take decisions on what to do	Execute	Disseminate results	When external support withdraws something
	Know them better	Decide on priorities	Improve	Ensure wide diffusion	concrete must remain
	Make them know you	Start up a schedule	Get interesting results		

Source: Stassart (1992) based on ETC (1992)

Amanor (1990) structured his analytical abstracts around the CIMMYT model of the steps in on-farm research that is: (i) diagnosis, (ii) planning, (iii) experimentation, (iv) analysis, (v) recommendation and follow up (Figure 4.1). Van der Bliek and van Veldhuizen (1993) and Stassart (1992) made use of the framework originally developed by ILEIA for promoting participatory agricultural projects (ETC, 1992). This framework describes a five-phase process which includes, (i) getting started, (ii) identifying options and making choices, (iii) improving and innovating (trying out new activities), (iv) spreading out, and (v) sustaining the process (Table 4.1).

The second approach is one which focuses on the level, character or mode of participation in a programme or activity, and perhaps the best-known example is Biggs's (1989) framework, which categorizes participation as either (i) contractual, (ii) consultative, (iii) collaborative or (iv) collegiate (see Figure 2.3). Farrington and Bebbington (1993) enlarged on the approach taken by Biggs, and categorized programmes according to the 'depth of farmer participation', by making use of categories similar to those of Biggs, but including some reference to implementation strategies, such as whether the programme works with individuals or groups. At the same time they included a second axis which divides programmes according to the scope of their subject matter: whether they have a narrow, specifically agricultural focus, or cover a wide variety of activities.

For the purpose of this review two criteria are also used to classify approaches to the implementation of farmer participatory research. First a distinction is made in terms of the larger programme context within which the farmer participatory research activities take place (Figure 4.2). Three general categories of programme context can be identified, including (i) broad community development programmes, (ii) agricultural development programmes focused specifically on farmer participatory research, and (iii) agricultural research programmes. This distinction corresponds to that used by Farrington and Bebbington in the sense that community development programmes, by definition, are wide in scope whereas agricultural development and agricultural research activities are generally more focused. This dimension is important because of the impact it has on the priority given to farmer participatory research. Where it is implemented within a general development programme, farmer participatory research is usually a minor activity attracting a minimum of resources. The examples that follow, therefore, largely refer to activities taking place in the context of either agricultural development or research programmes.

The second, and perhaps more important axis follows Richards (1985) in distinguishing between two broad approaches to interacting with farmers' informal research and development activities. The first is a minimal strategy whereby a 'space' is maintained between farmers' informal research and formal science, while the second is a more active, interventionist strategy that seeks to establish, support and expand farmers' research and development activities. The second axis, therefore, distinguishes between programmes and approaches involving more or less direct intervention in the farmers' own experimentation.[2]

Clearly any framework can be challenged as few projects or activities fit neatly within one category or another. Thus the idea was not to rigidly categorize the various examples of farmer participatory research programmes and activities on the basis of the framework. Rather, the framework is used as a general guide for the presentation and analysis of the examples. Some considerable detail is presented concerning a limited number of examples which illustrate distinctly different approaches, while a number of others are presented in less detail. The remainder of the programmes and activities reviewed are presented within the discussion of issues in Chapter 5.

The programme context within which farmer participatory research takes place: community or general development programmes

In many ways this group of farmer participatory research activities is problematic in that community development programmes vary

---

[2] We use the term 'intervention' in the sense defined by Röling and de Zeeuw (1983:32): 'A systematic effort to strategically apply resources to manipulate seemingly causal elements in an ongoing social process, so as to permanently reorient the process in directions deemed desirable by the intervening party'. The framework reflects an early discussion by Olivier de Sardan (1990) who points to the balance between development implying local populations taking charge and external intervention involving the transfer of knowledge and resources.

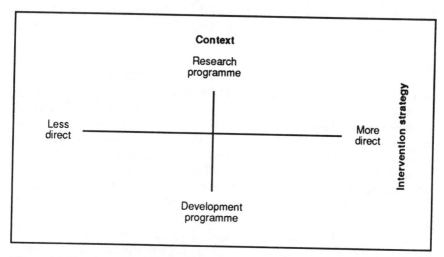

Figure 4.2 *Framework for the classification of approaches to the implementation of farmer participatory research*

considerably in scope, and in general, implementation strategies have not been determined by any specific consideration of the agricultural research activities itself. Thus, the structure and organization of most of these programmes, including site and client selection, do not reflect a specific concern to work within, strengthen or establish a particular research process within communities, or the need to investigate particular agricultural problems within a participatory research framework. The subordinate nature of most research that takes place within broader community development programmes has meant that it is particularly difficult, using documentation alone, to organize and analyse in any systematic manner the specific experiences with farmer participatory research. However, the recent series of studies and publications by ODI on the relationships between NGOs and agricultural technology development provide some useful insights (Farrington and Lewis, 1993; Bebbington and Thiele, 1993; Wellard and Copestake, 1993). In addition, Cromwell and Wiggins (1993) reviewed the particular area of seed research and supply by non-government organizations. All these authors conclude that relatively few development organizations or programmes devote a significant proportion of their total resources to agricultural research. For example, with respect to the 18 organizations with seed projects reviewed by Cromwell and Wiggins, only two agencies supported local seed systems as their primary activity. For the majority, research relating to seed was an adjunct to existing development programmes, and only half the agencies employed agriculturalists or specialist seed staff to implement their seed work.

On the other hand, the work of the few NGOs that do have an established research interest is often similar in orientation to that of much conventional research, and a number of these NGOs actually have their own research stations. Some of the largest and most well established of these are in Asia, and Farrington and Lewis (1993) have detailed a number of examples of their successful technology development activities: FIVBD adapted and established its own hatchery; BAIF developed a technique for freezing semen for artificial insemination; RDRS in Bangladesh developed a treadle pump; and PRADAN developed less sophisticated sterilization techniques for mushroom production. In addition, some of these organizations developed new forms of social ownership to benefit poorer groups: BRAC is now widely known for the introduction of women para-veterinarians and Proshika for its programme to make irrigation equipment available to landless people who were then in a position to sell water to land owners.

Nevertheless, the research perspective, while being problem oriented, in many cases was not particularly participatory. Hence, with respect to the improved mushroom production technique developed by PRADAN, Farrington and Lewis note that 'the change agent had to spend 3 to 6 months working with local groups to elicit their interest in the technology, to identify their actual and potential levels of capability and to allow them to own the idea.' On the other hand, the work of ATA in Thailand appears to sit at the other end of the participatory continuum in that it focused on identifying existing examples of rice-fish technology, with the operators of these systems becoming resource people who could share their experiences with others. This theme of participation through shared information is also evident with respect to ATA's work on pest control methods already in use by farmers, which was assembled, published and disseminated both within and beyond Thailand. The FIVDB duck-rearing programme in Bangladesh is also involved in assembling farmer knowledge for wider dissemination. Similar examples can be found in ODI's Latin American case studies where organizations have focused their work on the incorporation of local knowledge into research: NGOs diagnose situations, evaluate current practices and subsequently elaborate technologies which combine farmer knowledge with 'elements of practices the NGO aims to introduce.' Thus, CAAP carried out research on native crops and pest control using different rotation systems, FBU has been involved in screening indigenous technology and CESA has used indigenous soil surveys. A similar example from the Africa case studies is that of ENDA which has given considerable attention to the collection of local crop germplasm.

At the same time, most organizations carrying out farmer participatory research within broader development programmes are involved in training farmers in certain production techniques and experimental methods. Trials and demonstrations implemented by farmers are, therefore, an important feature of many programmes. Farrington and Lewis, for example, refer to the operations of the Mennonite Central Committee (MCC) which has a long history of research in Bangladesh, with on-farm trials implemented since the early 1970s. MCC programmes in Bangladesh have involved adaptive testing by co-operatives of different crops and the transfer of cultivation techniques from government and international research centres to farmers' fields. BAIF carried out similar tests. Other organizations such as Auroville have used experimental stations to train farmers in the use of particular technologies. A similar situation is reported for NGOs operating within Africa: at least until the late 1980s, most research themes were initiated by the organizations themselves and subsequently passed to farmers for testing and/or adoption under a fairly well-defined programme (see Wellard and Copestake (1993) for examples, including the Langbesi Agricultural Station in Northern Ghana, the Gwembe Valley Agricultural Mission in Zambia and the CARE Agroforestry Extension Project in Kenya). There is, however, evidence of some recent change in orientation. In 1989, CRS in The Gambia changed its policy and placed all agronomic work including conventional varietal and fertilizer trials, which had previously been carried out on station, on farmers' fields. Currently, CRS is testing a pilot farmer participatory research programme which aims to build up, through training, farmers' capacities to experiment (Owens, 1993).

Gilbert (1990) and Sarch (1993) provide details of a 'farmer innovation and technology testing programme' initiated by the Gambian government research services with seven NGOs. The technologies under test and the design of the tests were determined by the government services. In addition, the tests were to be implemented through farmers' groups following the example of the ATIP programme in Botswana (Norman *et al.*, 1989), and in a number of cases, group plots were established. Bebbington and Thiele (1993) identify 20–30 NGOs in Latin America who are involved in similar kinds of testing and since 1990, CIAT in Colombia has been implementing 'participatory tests' with a number of NGOs.

Thus, in many respects, farmer participatory research activities taking place within broader development programmes have not moved much beyond the models and levels of participation which characterized farming systems research during the 1980s. With reference to the framework of Biggs, they have made little progress in moving from contractual to collegial relationships in their agricultural research activities. Nevertheless, there are, as previously indicated, some exceptions. ATA moved onto farmers' fields for further testing after identifying farmers' own pest control methods, and CRS is also proposing to do so. In Central America, CIPRES and ADRO are described as having urged farmer collaborators to design their own informal experiments with ideas or materials provided through the programmes. While not focused specifically on participatory research, it is interesting that the recent ODI reviews place much emphasis on the very active role being played by the organizations themselves, rather than farmers, in the research process.

While Bebbington and Thiele (1993) note that NGO agricultural research activities do not appear to differ significantly from those implemented by agricultural research institutions, they argue that NGOs are more sensitive to local organizations and, in general, are interested and active in organizational strengthening and popular education with a view to community mobilization and empowerment. Thus, common to many of the development programmes which have a farmer participatory research component are explicit objectives in terms of the empowerment of local communities. In their discussion of Central American NGOs, for example, Bebbington and Thiele refer to the NGOs' 'alternative development' approach as being more about process than specific technologies. These processes include popular education, farmer organization, farmer experimentation and participatory diagnosis. While these concerns appear to be particularly strong in Latin America, the detailed case study of Silveira House in Zimbabwe provides an example of this approach in Africa (Wellard and Copestake, 1993). While Silveira House is not known for its particular concern with the sustainability of the technology which it promotes, it is known for its skills in community organization. Cromwell and Wiggins (1993) suggest that this is also true of many of the seed projects they reviewed: for many organizations, seeds are seen as part of a strategy for helping farmers to recover a measure of control by offering alternatives to the standard, chemical-dependent packages provided by formal sector agencies.

The programme context within which farmer participatory research takes place: agricultural development and agricultural research programmes

Outside the context of broader development programmes there are two more or less distinct groups of farmer participatory research programmes: (i) those which use farmer participation as a research tool for very specific problems, and (ii) those which address agricultural research as a long-term, community-based development process. In the case of the former group, a number of considerations associated with sustaining a long-term, local process of innovation, do not feature. On the other hand, considerations concerning the selection of appropriate research partners feature prominently. Both types of programme can be implemented with varying degrees of intervention.

Among the examples presented below, there are three which use farmer participation essentially as tool in the context of an agricultural research programme (Agricultural Technology Improvement Project [ATIP] – Botswana; Crop-fish systems research in Malawi, Bangladesh and Ghana; and the varietal selection programmes in Rwanda and Nepal) and seven involving farmer participatory research in the context of agricultural development programmes (Community-based Management of Tsetse Control – Kenya; Participatory Agricultural Research and Extension Project [PAREP] India; Participatory Research and Extension Project [PREP] – Rwanda; Farmers' Research Project [FRP] Ethiopia; FarmLink Project – Egypt; Chivi Food Security Project – Zimbabwe; Sustainable Agriculture and Village Extension Project [SAVE] – Sierra Leone; Farmers Participatory Research Project [FPRP] – Uganda). Among these, some use direct intervention and training strategies while others use less direct strategies (Table 4.2). For clarity of presentation the examples are grouped and presented in the following sections according to the level of intervention. At the same time, each case has been selected to demonstrate particular issues discussed in much of the farmer participatory research literature.

More direct intervention

The Participatory Research and Extension Project, COOPIBO, Rwanda[3]

The COOPIBO project aims to improve the dialogue between the formal and informal research systems and to organize institutional structures to transform the agrarian economy and improve rural welfare. The case has been selected to highlight its central feature, the establishment of cyclical group innovation processes based on the annual cropping cycle.

The programme began in 1987 with a conventional, 'sophisticated' farming systems analysis controlled by researchers. By 1989 the initial programme had failed and a second process involving participatory workshops was initiated which resulted in proposals for a programme to support the dynamics of informal research. The main concern of the project has been to develop and sustain a continuous process of group innovation. Programme documentation emphasizes that technical concerns in terms of farmer research and participatory extension can only be addressed over time when the groups reach 'maturity'.

The groups themselves are described as 'interest groups', and are formed to address particular topics, such as vegetable gardening or goat production. Some of the groups are based on pre-existing groups or structures (e.g., mutual savings and aid groups), but others are new, formed specifically for 'project'-sponsored activities (or when a previous

---

[3] Information drawn from Stassart and Mukandakasa (1992).

Table 4.2 Characteristics of example farmer participatory research programmes

Project	Acronym	Agency	Country	Programme context	Intervention strategy
Agricultural Technology Improvement Project	ATIP	National government	Botswana	Research	More direct
Rice-fish culture		ICLARM	Malawi, Ghana and Bangladesh	Research	More direct
Community Tsetse Trapping		ICIPIE	Kenya	Research	More direct
Crop variety selection		National government and CIAT	Nepal and Rwanda	Research	More direct
Participatory Agricultural Research and Extension Project	PAREP	KRIBHCO	India	Development	More direct
Participatory Research and Extension Project	PREP	COOPIBO	Rwanda	Development	More direct
Farmers Research Project	FPR	Farm Africa	Ethiopia	Development	More direct
FarmLink	Farm Link	CARE	Egypt	Development	Less direct
Chivi Food Security Project	Chivi	ITDG	Zimbabwe	Development	Less direct
Sustainable Agriculture and Village Extension Project	SAVE	CARE	Sierra Leone	Development	Less direct
Farmers Participatory Research Project	FPRP	ActionAid	Uganda	Development	Less direct

activity, such as vegetable gardening, was initiated). Individuals may be members of more than one group.

Not all group members are equally involved in training and research. Rather, group representatives are elected by members and they receive training for onward transmission to the group as a whole. An example is given of market gardening groups who elect 'collecting farmers' to grow new types of vegetables. These elected farmers are designated as 'experts' who are encouraged and trained to be farmer-researchers and play a role in extension: they, therefore, need to be able to transmit the results of their research to the group.

This project places considerable emphasis on exchange visits between farmers and researchers and amongst the farmers themselves. Seminars and workshops focused on specific technical problems such as animal diseases are key to the exchange of information between the different partners. Designated expert farmers also visit experiment stations. A case is cited of three women farmers delegated to visit the Institute of Agronomic Sciences to select bean varieties, an activity that is termed the 'stage of discovery'.[4] These visits are followed by subsequent 'research and adaptation stages.' The programme sees itself as 'becoming a communication service, stimulating exchanges and organizing the interaction to allow farmers to discover potential solutions that exist and are practised elsewhere.'

Improvements in group management of activities are achieved through familiarization with the programme planning cycle – proposal, assessment, execution, follow-up, programming, etc. – which occurs annually. Over time, as the groups mature, they are expected to be able to apply their research skills to other technical and non-technical topics. While emphasis is placed on this group process, the individual groups are not necessarily viewed as permanent: they may disappear as new groups are formed. Since individuals are often members of more than one group, the overall experience is expected to be transferable and hence, to be adaptable to a range of different subjects and situations.

Farmers' Research Project, Farm Africa, Ethiopia[5]

Farm Africa's participatory research project in the North Omo Zone in the south-west of Ethiopia was initiated in February 1991. The project has been selected because of its particular structural features and the emphasis placed on linking non-government and government organizations and farmers. In this project, Farm Africa, a UK-based NGO, works as a

---

[4] This aspect of the project is part of CIAT's collaborative programme.

[5] Material for this case was largely taken from Sandford (1990), Farm Africa (1991) and Biggs and Pound (1992).

service organization rather than project implementor. The project is implemented by collaborating NGOs for whom agriculture is only one component of their activities. While the programme emphasizes increasing the flow of technical information in the hands of both researchers and farmers, considerable attention is given to the training of farmers in the establishment of on-farm trials as part of its strategy to link farmers and researchers.

The project aims to close the gap between formal research, farmers and non-governmental organizations in order to increase the ability of NGOs with agricultural development programmes to make a more effective contribution to community-resourced, farmer-operated research. The project plans to achieve this by providing these organizations access to existing research experience (by opening lines of communication), helping test research results and by investigating and encouraging farmers' own innovation. The project was, therefore, conceived of as providing a service to other organizations already operating in the North Omo area. While it began by working with NGOs, the project has shifted over time to working more closely with government and formal research institutions.

Work began with a series of initial surveys to identify farming systems and constraints and to 'initiate and refine procedures for conducting constructive, two-way dialogue with representatives of all categories of farmers in a community.' An attempt was also made to identify 'farmer experimenters' with whom the project might work.

The lack of relevant information on the main crops and activities in the zone is considered to be a key constraint to agricultural development. A key project activity, therefore, has been to fill gaps in existing technical information relevant to the farming systems in the area. In the case of at least one crop, ensete or false banana (*Ensete edulis*), this has primarily involved the recording of local knowledge since the crop has received relatively little attention from the formal research system. To date, the project has collated, published and circulated material on ensete and taro, and similar work is in progress for other crops.

As this was conceived of as a service project, training is a core activity involving both the staff of the non-government and government organizations, as well as farmers. Staff have been trained in rapid rural appraisal techniques, while farmer training has been directed towards increasing their understanding of the agricultural research process. Two approaches have been taken, one more formal in the sense of learning specific techniques and approaches. A central component of this work has been the establishment of a programme of trials for testing research results both at individual farmer and community levels. A second, less formal but equally structured training activity, involves visits to research stations and on-farm research activities in the zone. The farmer training is viewed as part of a strategy to improve dialogue between farmers and researchers. Unsuccessful attempts to identify experimenter farmers led to the abandonment of the plan to encourage and monitor farmers' own innovation.

Little indication is given in the documentation of the types of farmers actually involved in the activities. This reflects the fact that Farm Africa itself serves only as a link organization: farmer selection for trials is done by the NGOs implementing the programme rather than the researchers or Farm Africa. Selected participants may also be involved in other unrelated activities. Joint farmer/researcher activities have been limited to the initial constraints, identification surveys and some involvement in the identification of the subject matter for trials. Farmers were not involved in the analysis or dissemination of findings from the diagnostic surveys.

Some changes in approach have been necessary following the project's initial experiences. For example, formal research institutions have become more central to the programme as a number of NGOs were unable, due to the demands of their other activities, to give the time and resources required. In addition, little attention has been given to farmer experimentation: as indicated above, little on-going farmer experimentation was identified. Finally, Farm Africa has itself become more directly involved in carrying out trials in order to gain additional experience with the technologies and experimental methods.

Farmer Participatory Research Project, ActionAid/NRI, Uganda[6]
The key objective of the ActionAid Farmer Participatory Research Project in Uganda is to complement existing farmer capacity to experiment by enhancing farmers' skills and understanding of experimental methods. Like the Farm Africa programme outlined above, this project is interesting because of its particular structural arrangements. The programme was started in 1992 by ActionAid, a NGO, in co-operation with the Natural Resources Institute (NRI), a British government research and development organization. While it lies within ActionAid's integrated development project addressing community defined problems within agriculture, health, water and sanitation, education, literacy and road improvement, the agricultural research component has been placed within a separate Farmer Participatory Research Unit which is partly staffed by appointees of the NRI, which also provides some technical backstopping. The purpose of the Unit is to investigate, develop and test appropriate methodologies for promoting active farmer participation in research. At

---

[6] Material for this case was taken from the project proposal (ActionAid Uganda/NRI, 1992), a quarterly report of the Farmer Participatory Research Unit (ActionAid Uganda/NRI, 1993) and from discussions with A. Martin.

the field level, this Unit works through ActionAid staff who are also involved in other activities.

The agricultural programme began with a period of PRA-based diagnostic work in selected villages where other ActionAid programmes were already being implemented. This resulted in the identification of key problem areas for future research, including cassava diseases (especially cassava mosaic) and soil fertility. In principle the Farmer Participatory Research Unit is concerned with 'problem-solving experiments' and determining the appropriate timing and method of intervention to improve farmers' experimental techniques: the programme is only in its first year of operation and techniques are still being developed. In general, the Unit works with groups of farmers that are selected by the ActionAid field staff. The Unit has been particularly concerned with the issue of the relevance of farmer participatory approaches in areas where farmers have little knowledge. Much of the work to date has involved the evaluation of cassava varieties for tolerance to cassava mosaic. The farmers and researchers together determine the objectives and design of the trials.

Agricultural Technology Improvement Project (ATIP), Botswana[7]
This project provides an example of a participatory research programme based on farmer groups working within the context of a government research institution. In this case, the groups were formed specifically for the research task and the programme is independent of any other development activities. While the programme was designed to meet the specific objective of improving the output of the formal research and extension system, it was also expected that low-cost methods for on-farm research and extension would be developed.

ATIP began in 1982 with a classical, interdisciplinary, farming systems perspective: individual farmers were involved primarily through 'researcher managed' trials with the goal of identifying improved arable crop production technologies. In order to increase the level of involvement of farmers in technology development and the range of farmers involved, a programme of farmer managed trials implemented through research-oriented farmer groups was initiated from 1985–86. Over time, the programme has developed the group concept and now distinguishes between different types of research groups according to their role in technology development. Extension groups responsible for dissemination and monitoring have also been added, which are involved in local testing of a limited number of 'recommended' technologies.

Although on-farm trials are central to the programme and an important focus for research group discussions, the groups were formed in order to

---

[7] The experience of the Agricultural Technology Improvement Project (ATIP) Botswana is taken from Worman *et al.* (1988, 1989), Heinrich *et al.* (1991) and Heinrich (1993).

60

create an opportunity for a continuing dialogue between researchers and farmers about production problems and opportunities as well as for presenting trial results and making future plans. The dialogue takes place at routine meetings, held in some cases on a monthly basis. It is this process of dialogue which is viewed as the key to the success of the approach. While the groups are used to help establish a work plan, improve trial implementation rates and reduce errors, all trials are conducted on an individual basis. The groups are involved in discussion of technical options presented by researchers, and farmers who select the same options form sub-groups for conducting trials. Within the different research groups farmers are seen as having a variable amount of control over the research agenda. However, standard trial designs which are reported to meet the needs of both researchers and farmers are used. Research field staff assist with trials by laying out plots, ensuring that plant types and densities are uniform and assessing plot yields.

Crop–fish systems research in Malawi, Bangladesh and Ghana [8]
The case of integrated agriculture and aquaculture systems under investigation by ICLARM, a member of the CGIAR, is used to demonstrate the low-external input concerns of farmer participatory research and the potential use of PRA tools by producers themselves. The focus of ICLARM's work is the development of new ways of farming through biological diversification and nutrient recycling. ICLARM is one of the few formal research institutions for which the development of sustainable whole farm systems is the central objective. Achievement of this objective depends on detailed agro-ecosystems analysis which is completed with the full participation of farmer colleagues and collaborating national research programmes using participatory mapping and modelling as management tools.

Lightfoot and Noble describe a research programme initiated in Malawi in 1990, the objective of which was to enable farmers to develop their own crop–fish systems. Currently farmers practice rice and fish production as separate enterprises. Steps in the research process are described, including visits by farmers to the National Aquaculture Research Station to see demonstrations of integrated rice–fish systems. The process began with modelling workshops on farms during which farmers themselves prepared flow models of household resources. Subsequently, workshops were held during which an experiment station was visited and a series of farmer-designed systems discussed. With no further input from the researchers, these farmers, and 40 others who did

---

[8]   The information on the crop-fish systems has been extracted from the following sources: Lightfoot *et al.* (1992) for Bangladesh; Lightfoot and Noble (1992) for Malawi and Ofori *et al.* (1993) for Ghana.

not attend the workshop, are reported to have experimented with and developed their own unique crop–fish production systems. The authors emphasize the minimal involvement of researchers in the process and the ease with which farmers are able to manage the development tools: the experimentation developed out of an inexpensive one-day modelling and mapping workshop and a one-day demonstration of the technology on station.

The Malawi experience repeats similar work in Bangladesh and Ghana where, through repeated visits to farms and research stations, the culture of short-cycle fish species in underutilized seasonal ponds and ditches, fed largely with on-farm wastes, has been developed. In all cases, the participatory research programme began with brainstorming sessions using models of existing and future flows of farm resources, and followed directly with farmer experimentation. The models on which the programmes are based are used in a continuous process of systems monitoring and evaluation by the farmers themselves.

Participatory Agricultural Research and Extension Project, Krishak Bharati Co-operative Ltd (KRIBHCO), Eastern India[9]

While this project is focused on agricultural technology development, like the PREP programme in Rwanda, considerable emphasis has been placed on the development of a sustainable community-level process of problem analysis, research and extension. In this case, however, emphasis is placed on community rather than group processes. The project draws on the experiences of NGOs as well as the Rainfed Farming Project in Eastern India (funded by ODA and implemented by the Hindustan Fertilizer Corporation).

The objectives of the project are:

> to develop and implement a poverty-focused (poor families to be given priority), participatory (joint problem diagnosis through the use of participatory rural appraisal techniques) approach to agricultural research and development ... which is sustainable (a local capability is created to continue provision of services after the project) and replicable, and to improve the livelihood of poor families by making appropriate technologies available to them.

The project emphasizes the use of a participatory planning approach within which target villages are fully involved in the planning of activities they wish to implement in their communities. The overall planning process begins with a very general participatory rural appraisal,

---

[9] Material for this case was largely taken from the report of a project preparation mission between the University of Wales and KRIBHCO (KRIBHCO, 1992).

which is followed by community problem analysis and the identification of development options and priorities. As a final step a village workplan is developed.

In the preliminary programme document emphasis was placed on the sustainability of any project-initiated action, and thus on the design of a viable system of problem analysis and agenda setting which could be maintained beyond the life of the project. This is to be achieved through training of key community members and the establishment of local institutions. It is the local institution-building process which has attracted considerable attention by donors.

Although the programme will eventually be maintained by the communities themselves, initially, community development workers are being used to implement the programme. One of their tasks is to identify and record traditional knowledge and practices, provide feedback for planning, organize agricultural demonstrations and facilitate meetings. They act as village animators until individuals from within the villages have been identified and trained to take over these motivating and facilitating tasks. It is assumed that the local animators will ultimately be directly employed by the communities concerned and will, therefore, be accountable to them.

At the same time as these institution-building processes are ongoing, the project seeks to achieve its technical objectives by working directly with farmers to support their own trials and experimentation. The project also includes activities to strengthen state agricultural universities.

Community Tsetse Trapping, ICIPE, Kenya[10]
This adaptive research programme is being implemented by the International Centre for Insect Physiology and Ecology (ICIPE) with support from NRI, and is located in the Lambwe Valley of Western Kenya. The case provides an example of a formal research institution introducing a technology which depends on community organization and participation for its success. Thus, while the project is ultimately concerned with the control of tsetse, two years after starting, the technology has not yet been put in place.

The goal is to develop environmentally sound tsetse control technologies, and it is one of a number of institutions which have been involved in tsetse control over many years. Over time, control strategies have evolved from the use of insecticidal sprays to control tsetse over extensive areas, to traps and targets which depend on more intensive, local management. As part of this shift from external implementation of technology to more participative control systems, ICIPE established a Social Science Interface Unit which is playing a lead role in this

---

[10] Sources: ICIPE, 1992/3.

multidisciplinary programme. The programme is working with local communities and local government institutions to develop trap management systems and at the same time to monitor the effects of reduced tsetse challenge on land use, livestock and crop productivity. Like the ATIP programme in Botswana, ICIPE hopes to develop procedures for wider dissemination of the technology.

While the wider project objectives are to improve the welfare of communities in the tsetse-infested areas of Homa Bay District, Kenya, the specific objectives are to: identify options for community management of 'NGU' (odour-baited) traps; develop a monitoring plan covering livestock and crop production and community implementation and management skills; and develop extension tools and training modules for extension personnel involved in subsequent dissemination of the trap technology. Studies are currently being conducted in the use of similar trap odour-bait systems to control a wider range of tsetse species and it is expected that the experience with the NGU trap system will be particularly valuable.

Project activities to date have included location-specific baseline studies of community resources, livestock production and health, tsetse populations, and the current status of human sleeping sickness. Community mobilization has been promoted through training on tsetse biology, trap making and servicing, and the formation of organizations for planning, implementation and management of control systems. A monitoring programme has been developed to assess the efficacy of the organizational framework, and the impact of the control mechanisms on the tsetse population, tsetse-borne diseases (cattle trypanosomiasis and human sleeping sickness), livestock populations and land and crop productivity. In addition the monitoring activities will enable the calculation of the overall social and economic costs and benefits of this particular approach to tsetse control.

The key to the eventual success of this programme will be the participation of the local communities, and ICIPE has concentrated on facilitating community efforts to mobilize resources to develop and implement their own control strategy. As part of its contribution towards this mobilization, ICIPE trained a group of forty or so farmers who were in turn to mobilize their communities. This training involved the provision of detailed information on tsetse biology and ecology: the researchers are of the opinion that this knowledge will provide the incentive to continue to trap flies in spite of declining numbers appearing in the traps over time. An attempt was also made to assess the farmers' own knowledge about tsetse ecology and the way in which disease is transmitted, as this knowledge is central to the trap technology. Practical sessions in trap making, placement and maintenance were also included. The second training element concerned community organization, and the communities have been encouraged to form an organization with the specific task of implementing and maintaining a trapping programme. As noted above, it is currently assumed by researchers that successful fly control within the valley will depend on the involvement of a number of villages. Individual control is not considered to be an adequate solution although ultimately, this may be an important component. Since the training programme was completed the researchers have played the role of observers, intervening at community meetings only to provide information. Monitoring and evaluation activities are expected to continue on a long-term basis.

Less direct intervention
FarmLink Project, CARE, Egypt[11]
This project has as its central objective the linking of people regarded as having an important contribution to make to agricultural development. Project activities are highly focused and concentrate on making links and developing a monitoring programme which can be used for assessing the efficacy of the links. Unlike the previous cases involving NGOs, FarmLink is not part of a wider development programme.

The project is based on the assumption that Egypt has a wealth of agricultural technology and relevant information plus a large population of farmers who do not presently have access to it. Thus, it aims to link horticultural producers who want to experiment and innovate, with sources of agricultural information. The project makes no effort to encourage any particular technology or any particular way of assessing a technology, and researchers, input suppliers and farmers are included in the link activities (approximately 60 per cent of links made between farmers and sources of innovation are actually farmer-to-farmer links).

Participants are identified through a series of workshops which include groups of self-selected farmers from villages with which protocols have been established. Farmers must belong to the project's target population, which is defined as small, innovative farmers (large-scale farmers, and individuals who are not primarily farmers, are generally excluded). Workshops are used to identify linkage needs: they begin with broad statements of interest and end with a proposed package of link activities tailored for small groups of farmers with similar interests. These interests and needs are determined with the help of 'innovator analysis', a technique that uses flow charts to develop a SWOT-style[12] analysis. The

---

[11] Information about this project is taken from unpublished project documents provided by S. Woolsey, FarmLink Project Manager.

[12] A method of participatory analysis that identifies the Strengths, Weaknesses, Opportunities and Threats associated with a particular situation or intervention.

link programmes which follow involve a series of visits to different information sources, usually within the farmers' local area. Thus the link is, in principal, always repeatable. In this way, farmers are not only able to evaluate a new idea but also to establish a relationship with the new information source. The initial idea was that following link activities, farmers would design and implement small experiments on their own farms that incorporated the new ideas, varieties or techniques to which they were exposed during the link. Initially, considerable emphasis was placed on these trials. However, following a recent re-orientation, the project focus is now squarely on the linkage process itself. Thus, considerably more attention is now being given to the production of 'a quality interface' between farmers and technology: any subsequent experimental activities are in the hands of the farmers (Figure 4.3).

Chivi Food Security Project, ITDG, Zimbabwe[13]

This is the second example of a highly focused programme implemented by a NGO. As with FarmLink above, the project seeks to increase local food security through the provision of technical information and training to farmers which they can then use to carry out their own research. In contrast to FarmLink, however, this programme also seeks to strengthen existing local institutions. These activities do not, however, form part of a wider development programme. The project is less common for ITDG on two accounts: it is not focused on a specific technical theme, nor is it being implemented through another NGO.

The project was initiated in 1991 and is entirely focused on existing local groups: farmers' clubs and vegetable gardening groups for example, and local research and development organizations. This was considered essential to the future sustainability of any process initiated during the project. Participatory needs assessments are followed by visits to nearby research stations in order to expose farmers to a range of available options. ITDG merely acts as a facilitator in this process, as the participants determine what is of interest and what they would like to know more about. The project arranges for any subsequent training to be given by the relevant organization: however, no training is given on how to do trials, and farmers are simply left to do what they want. Training and implementation of options are followed by 'mini review workshops' focused on particular activities, possibly with someone from the research station. An exception to this non-interventionist approach is the encouragement given to groups to opt for 'Training for Transformation', the development education programme designed to increase self awareness and the ability to transform society (Hope and Timmel, 1991). This type of training is viewed by the project as an important catalyst for

---

[13] Based on information provided by C. Watson of ITDG.

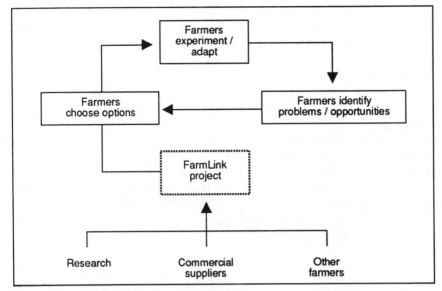

Source: FarmLink Evaluation Report (1992)

Figure 4.3 *Model of the Farmlink Project* Source: FarmLink Evaluation Report (1992)

subsequent events.

While the majority of activities occur at the level of farmer groups, the project is also concerned to influence local, district and provincial level extension staff. Individual staff members are encouraged to attend workshops, and in particular the Training for Transformation sessions. The project believes that any permanent change in the relationship between farmers and the formal sector will depend on attitudinal change among research and extension staff.

Sustainable Agriculture and Village Extension Project (SAVE), CARE, Sierra Leone[14]

The SAVE project was launched by CARE in 1990 and aims to support local agriculture by the introduction of new crop planting material: the assumption is that farmers already have the interest and skills to experiment with new genetic material. As was the case with the FarmLink and Chivi programmes, activities have been focused almost entirely on improving the two-way flow of information between farmers and researchers, and amongst farmers themselves. 'Horizontal extension' is considered to be particularly important as there are few government

---

[14] Sources: Sumberg (1991) and George *et al.* (1992). It is also important to note that the project works in a district adjacent to the area studied by Richards (1985; 1986).

extension personnel in the project area.

The project simply supplies individual farmers with small quantities of seed or planting material of new varieties or new crops, with which they are encouraged to experiment. In order to facilitate the distribution of material, farmers must join associations, but these associations serve no other project purpose. Short courses on experimentation were initially planned but subsequently dropped and no other training or advice is given by the project extension staff (in fact, during its first three years SAVE had a strict, and controversial, policy against field agents giving any advice). The project simply serves as a link between farmers and researchers in order to improve the relevance of research activities. Since there is no research station in the vicinity and hence routine visits both to and from stations are not possible, farmers are monitored as to what they actually do with the planting material and these reactions are reported back to the researchers by CARE staff.

Crop variety selection programmes, Rwanda and Nepal[15]

These programmes are based on the premise that the ability of farmers to influence the research agenda depends on the early incorporation of farmer knowledge into research, rather than their involvement in testing previously developed technologies. The two programmes have been selected to demonstrate how some researchers are attempting to involve farmers in their research on experiment stations, which is often the starting point for agronomic research. The objectives of both programmes are more effective crop breeding and improved the returns to researcher time. Closer links are sought with farmers, but the farmers are not given any training since they are considered to already have the required knowledge.

The Rwanda programme began by focusing on questions relating to the strength of two 'knowledge systems', farmers and researchers. Thus, the Rwanda national bean research programme aims to identify widely adapted cultivars to accommodate large-scale, centralized seed production. Selection criteria focus only on yield characteristics and disease resistance. Thus from 250 cultivars initially screened possibly only two or three may eventually be tested under farm conditions. Farmer feedback is sought only after a five to seven year selection sequence at which time the cultivars are essentially finished products. In contrast, farmers themselves seek specific varieties for a range of production niches, and at least fifteen criteria are used. Using a more participatory approach combining the strengths of both partners, farmers ('bean experts') are involved in the selection process itself, which results in a larger number

---

[15] The information for Rwanda is taken from CIAT (1992), Scheideggar *et al.* (1991) and Sperling *et al.* (1993), and for Nepal from Thepa *et al.* (1992).

of cultivars being retained than if researchers alone were making the selections. This approach has allowed breeders to distinguish between two different categories of traits: preference and performance. These same bean experts perform their own on-farm tests using the selected cultivars. No direction is given regarding the manner in which these tests are performed.

Since 1990, the participatory research programme has concentrated on organizational questions: 'Could adaptive testing be completely devolved to farming communities? Could links between the informal and formal system become routine so that the results of farmers' own experimentation feeds back to the national programmes?' Reflecting these concerns, community groups were asked to send delegates to work on station, rather than the bean experts selected by the researchers, so that the farmers would have greater control over the research process. A report from the wheat breeding programme at the Pakhribas Agricultural Centre, Nepal provides a similar example. Thepa *et al.* (1992) describe the involvement for the first time of a random selection of men and women in the evaluation of wheat breeding lines at the experiment station, the first step in a planned participatory research process which resembles the five-step programme described by Mauriya *et al.* (1988). The main objective of the station evaluation is to incorporate farmers' selection criteria, and a comparison is made between the criteria used by men and those used by women, and between small-, medium- and large-scale farmers (in terms of their land resources). It is expected that the next step will be an analysis of farmers' own genetic material by breeders and a matching of these with researcher material will be followed by farmer testing and evaluation.

Summary

In this chapter a number of examples have been presented which illustrate the variety of operational approaches being taken to the implementation of farmer participatory research. Thus, activities referred to under the rubric of farmer participatory research may put more or less emphasis on the 'participatory' and 'research' aspects of the activities. We argue that these approaches reflect the differences in the broader ideological, institutional and programme contexts in which the farmer participatory research activities take place. One critical point that emerges from the review is the contrast among the examples in the level and mode of intervention. This variation in implementation approach has important implications for our understanding of the theoretical – and rhetorical – bases of farmer participatory research. These implications are explored in more detail in Chapters 5 and 6.

The examples also highlight several key issues that are addressed in the following chapters, including the role of participatory problem diagnosis, the kinds of information needed prior to programme implementation, the role and structure of agronomic trials in farmer participatory research and the selection and organization of trial participants.

5 Key Issues in Implementation

AS HIGHLIGHTED IN the previous chapters, farmer participatory research is seen as contributing to a wide range of outcomes or outputs, from those as broadly stated as empowerment, through the establishment of a sustainable local research capability, to the development and testing of specific technologies. Thus activities which are part of a broader community development programme are more likely to be framed and implemented in terms of social, political and institutional issues and objectives. Projects and activities which take place in an agricultural development framework are more likely to be concerned with establishing a long-term process of innovation within communities. Finally, agricultural research programmes that use participatory methods to enhance on-going activities may be interested in establishing a research partnership which will result in the development of more relevant technology. In each case, as was suggested by the examples presented in Chapter 4, the issues are distinctly different and present a range of complex operational decisions.

This chapter focuses on a number of these critical issues. First, the question of the selection of participants is addressed in relation to concerns about equity. The strategies of farmer participatory research programmes are then explored in terms of the sustainability of the processes of change which they hope to initiate. Brief reference is also made to issues surrounding the current interest in the use of agro-ecological approaches. Next, the focus is on the type of information needed prior to the implementation of research activities, whether they take place in the context of agricultural development or research programmes. The chapter ends with an introduction to the question of how farmer participatory research might be used to best advantage where human and material resources – on the part of both farmers and researchers – are scarce. While this chapter continues to refer to the examples presented in Chapter 4, some new material and examples are also introduced.

The selection of participants

There can be no doubt that a major issue for farmer participatory research programmes concerns the selection of participants. While the question of village selection appears to receive relatively less attention in the context of farmer participatory research than it did in farming systems research, strategies and criteria for the selection of individual farmers continue to be a major preoccupation. Participation in on-farm research can involve many different arrangements, models and levels of engagement, which have direct implications in terms of the selection of participants. In addition, not everyone in a community or location wishes or will be able to participate in research activities. Apart from these factors, it is clear that most communities show significant levels of differentiation in regard to education, wealth and access to and control of resources, and although there is little reliable information, it seems likely that communities are also differentiated in terms of innovative behaviour and 'research mindedness'. Thus, who participates in the research process has ramifications for the wider concerns of many projects – equity, social development, empowerment and sustainability – and can be expected to have a direct impact on the immediate research activities.

Broadly, two alternative selection strategies which reflect the often competing research and empowerment objectives of farmer participatory research, are employed. The first is to select innovative farmers who are rarely viewed as representative of any particular category of producers, although there is often an implicit assumption that they are resource rich. The rationale for their selection is that they can relatively easily share their knowledge with researchers. Gender may be considered in this selection process. The second alternative involves the selection of those considered to be best placed to represent their communities. Among the examples presented in Chapter 4, both strategies are evident.

One of the key debates in the farming systems literature revolved around the selection of villages (communities) and farmers to participate in on-farm trials. This related partly to the concern to identify relatively homogeneous 'recommendation domains', and many programmes classified villages and households in terms of, for example, the farming system or level of mechanization. Similar discussions continue in relation to participatory research, with distinctions being made between 'experimentation' and 'validation' trials (McCorkle, 1990). It has been suggested that the people involved in these would not necessarily be the same. Each of Biggs's modes of participation would also seem to demand different types of research partners (Table 5.1).

Such choices are being made by almost all farmer participatory research projects and not exclusively in relation to trials. It has been argued more generally that since the objective of farmer participatory research is to enhance the effectiveness and impact of both formal and informal research, trial participants should be the most 'research-minded'

Table 5.1 Types of farmers in relation to different modes of farmer participation in agricultural research

	Mode of participation			
	Contract	Consultative	Collaborative	Collegial
Type of farmer involved	Those who can guarantee the conditions of the contract	Representatives of the client group (which is defined by the scientists)	Representatives of client groups (which are jointly defined by scientists and farmers) and change over time; research minded farmers	Research minded farmers from the informal R & D system

Source: Biggs (1989)

individuals (Biggs and Pound, 1992).[1] A number of the national research programmes reviewed earlier by Biggs (1989) were attempting to select on this basis (e.g. Dual-Purpose Livestock Project in Panama; Small Ruminant Project in Indonesia; BARI in Bangladesh; Technology Testing Unit in Guatemala). Among the programmes discussed in Chapter 4, FarmLink refers to participants as 'innovator farmers', and the Rwanda bean programme sought to involve 'bean experts'. However, the selection of innovators or 'research-minded' individuals (or groups) is not straightforward. FarmLink project staff have voiced concerns: are innovator farmers really innovators? and, can a useful distinction be made between demonstrator farmers, who follow the protocol, and innovators, who actively manipulate new ideas? Johnson (1972) in an early treatment of farmers' own experimentation posed a similar question: what individual differences distinguish experimenters from conformists? These questions resemble those asked about adopters and non-adopters and in the case of the adoption–diffusion model of Rogers (1962), led to a profusion of studies attempting to describe the characteristics of the different client groups.

How are programmes defining or identifying 'research-minded' or innovative farmers? Sperling (1992), in the context of the Rwandan bean selection programme, is one of the few who details the difficult process of selecting 'farmer experts'. She compares the common practice of community nomination of participants with the researchers' own specific objective which, in this case, was to identify women who were successful bean growers, who consciously experimented with new varieties and who

---

[1] P. Richards (personal communication) suggests that since so much research is now no longer the product of the 'lone, mad genius' but rather of the research manager/team leader, the relevant qualifying participatory criteria should be determined by the answer to the question 'What prepares farmers to serve on the research management team?'

were able to extrapolate beyond the conditions of their own farms. Once an initial selection was made according to these criteria, it was necessary to identify women who were reflective, could speak clearly and were not intimidated by the presence of men. Subsequently farms were visited and the final selection was based on evidence of commitment, innovation and good (according to local agricultural practice) field maintenance. Finally, permission was sought from each woman's spouse. An earlier description of a similar procedure is provided by Ashby (1987), with 'experts' being identified by the farmers themselves.

It is generally accepted that actual participants in trials and other research activities are a limited subset of the *potential* beneficiaries of the technology or development process, regardless of the actual strategy and criteria used in selection. It is also assumed that sharing between participants and beneficiaries is not automatic.[2] In order to address this problem and to satisfy the desire for equity, a number of projects promote sharing of information and other direct benefits by implementing trials through groups rather than individuals. Ashby (1992) argues that this problem can also be addressed during the participant selection process. She suggests that it is useful to distinguish firstly between participants who are representative of client groups and others who are not. Both categories of participants can then be assessed according to their orientation to the larger body potential beneficiaries. Two orientations are identified: broad and equitable, or narrow and inequitable (Table 5.2). In the latter case, the participant, while representative of the beneficiaries, is not expected to be an effective leader and would be unlikely to diffuse benefits. Equally, even some atypical or unrepresentative participants (such as 'research-minded' farmers?) might be broad and equitable in orientation, and hence pass on information and other benefits in return for client support. Few programmes, however, appear to give so much systematic attention to the selection of participants.

As previously stated, a number of projects work with groups rather than with individuals. In some of these cases, only representatives of the group actually receive training or visit researchers, and it is their responsibility to share the experience with other group members. This is the case with the COOPIBO programme in Rwanda, where the group essentially functions as part of the extension strategy. In other programmes, all group members are trained. The Participatory Research

---

[2]   The experience of one breeding programme suggests, however, that sharing is not simply a question of willingness or other personality and societal characteristics. Sperling and Loevinsohn (1993) have concluded from their work that it can easily take up to three years before people are in a position to share planting material because of the small quantity of seed associated with trials and the various production problems that may be encountered.

Table 5.2 Effects of orientation and type of participants on the distribution of benefits from farmer participatory research

Type of participant	Orientation of particants	
	Broad and equitable	Narrow and inequitable
Representative of client groups	Effective leadership or diffusion from like-to-like	Ineffective leadership and poor communication results in little diffusion of benefits
Not representative of client groups	Effective leadership delivers benefits in return for client support	Elite club monopolies benefits

Adapted from Ashby (1992)

in Agriculture Project (IPRA) at CIAT in Colombia implements on-farm trials through committees of experimenting farmers formed by producers' organizations (CIAT, 1991). These committees are taught the principles of controlled comparison, replication and random assignment of treatments, and they apply them when setting up and running their own trials. The World Neighbor's Peasant Farmer Agricultural Self-Development Project in Burkina Faso has a different approach in that it emphasizes the role of community-level organization in determining priorities, analyzing problems and seeking solutions (Gubbels, 1988).

Projects justify the formation and use of groups on a variety grounds, some of which have already been indicated. For SAVE in Sierra Leone, the farmers' clubs are simply used to facilitate the distribution of planting material, and group leaders help organize meetings, workshops and field days. Similarly, FarmLink also organizes its participating farmers into groups for very pragmatic reasons: the organization of linking activities for individuals is wasteful of resources. A group approach may also be necessitated by the type of technology involved, as is the case with the ICIPIE tsetse-trapping programme, although not many research programmes have had to justify group formation for this reason. Biggs and Pound (1992) expressed the hope that the Farm Africa project would address some community and group-based institutional innovations which would necessitate evaluating how groups manage common property resources through, for example, trials at the level of a peasant association. An example of such an approach is provided by Loevinsohn et al. (1993), who describe the search for appropriate models of co-operation vis-à-vis rice production in the highland valleys of Rwanda. Bebbington and Thiele (1993) refer to the installation of on-farm trials on collective land as 'creating space for joint action.'

A popular reason for group formation is to improve communication and the exchange of relevant information. While this approach is typically associated with NGOs, it is also recognized as valid by other types of institutions (see Ashby *et al.*, 1989, for example). Thus, the ATIP programme in Botswana has given considerable attention to the use of groups, and over the last three years groups have become increasingly important in the Zambia Adaptive Research programme (Drinkwater, 1992).

The criteria for the selection of group members poses the same problems as with individuals. Most groups are not specifically formed to include people who are known experimenters: rather, the groups are viewed as the means by which communities learn about the process of identifying, testing and implementing new ideas or practices. They are also a means by which people can be encouraged to control their own situation.[3] Many NGOs have an ideological predisposition towards group formation as the only way in which individuals can affect underlying problems (whether gaining access to land or having a direct impact on the research agenda), and groups have a preferred place within their participatory development projects.[4] This is also reflected to some extent in the approaches being taken by farmer participatory research projects. For many projects, therefore, the question of groups is much larger than issues relating to trials, sharing and dialogue. It is not clear, however, that all programmes have analysed the processes in which groups are engaged: most of the information reviewed on this subject was descriptive, outlining how the groups started, identified interesting ideas, tried them out, etc., very much following the framework developed by ILEIA (see ETC, [1992] and Table 4.1).

Stassart and Mukandakasa (1992) provide a particularly detailed analysis of COOPIBO's experience using groups for agricultural research. Their experience leads them to conclude that the viability of the approach depends on three critical factors: (i) the presence of dynamic farmers within the different groups, (ii) the circulation of information which is stimulated by the fact that some farmers belong to more than one group, and (iii) the fact that some activities of different groups are

---

[3] Referring to Participative Technology Development (PTD), van der Bliek and van Veldhuizen (1993, p.6) argue that the PTD practitioner 'tries to link up with and strengthen the farmers' research process by making technology development a collective process and systematically developing the research process with farmers.'

[4] This view is not restricted to NGOs. Röling (1988) argues that an effective extension system depends on the presence of an active constituency, which interacts and networks. Amongst resource-poor farmers in less potential areas, intervention to create such a constituency – to create farmers' organizations – is necessary.

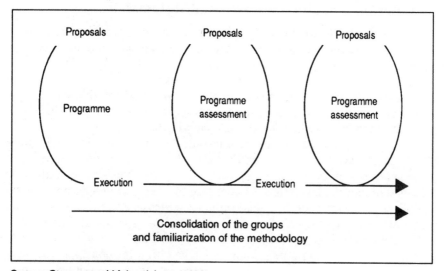

Source: Stassart and Mukandakasa (1992)

Figure 5.1 *Consolidation of groups by reflection/action cycles*

complementary. Their analysis acknowledges that just getting the group
'to work' is a major task which necessarily precedes innovative research
and extension activities. They observe that:

> ...some groups reach a maturity stage, where they progressively control
> the different stages of the cycle (proposals, programming, assessment,
> new proposals...) while at the same time integrating certain
> innovations'... (the next step is) 'supporting informal research in a
> more systematic way within the group and encouraging the extension
> of results to all its members ... so that the members themselves would
> be capable of solving future problems within their group *or in other*
> *farmer structures* (Figure 5.1).

The experience of the COOPIBO project in Tanzania suggests that groups
that are small in size with members who have close mutual relationships,
a common background and joint economic activities, are more likely to
be 'healthy' (i.e., survive long-term) (Galema and Mzigani, 1992). From
their comparison of trials carried out by farmer associations and co-
operatives, Loevinsohn *et al.* (1993) conclude that the ease of
organizational innovation supporting irrigated rice in the highland valley
areas reflected the relative evenness with which benefits were distributed
within the groups. What is particularly interesting about the COOPIBO
project in Rwanda is the fact that the groups are not viewed as permanent
and unchanging: what is depicted is a complex, changing network rather
than a rigid structure.

Farmer participatory research and sustainability

The sustainability of processes introduced through farmer participatory research and their long-term impact of projects are a major concern. Clearly there are a number of ways in which these questions can be addressed. At one level the attention given to the sustainability of processes simply reflects the nature of the frameworks within which most projects (whether focused on farmer participation or not) take place. It is suggested, for example, that the last step in the project process, and the key to sustainability, is to demonstrate to 'communities' (via their representatives or selected participants) how to manage 'the project' themselves and even apply for further funding. Nevertheless, there is long-standing evidence that outsiders (in the sense of people not directly affected by the project) or outside contact serves as a significant stimulant to processes of change, such as innovative or experimental behaviour. Thus, on returning to a project after it had officially 'closed', one NGO observed that although the groups which had been formed appeared to be intact, and previously introduced activities were ongoing, no new initiatives had been taken since the departure of project employees (S. Croxton, personal communication).

One strategy to secure sustainability is to seek to minimize dependence on the project. Thus, exchange visits between communities and local research stations are an important activity in a large proportion of the projects cited, and cross-community visits are limited to the immediate geographical area. The FarmLink Project is concerned to ensure that innovator farmers who participate in link activities have enough information (names, addresses and telephone numbers) to enable them to make contact and visits themselves at a later date. As part of its strategy, SAVE specifically instructed its field staff not to provide general guidance or instructions on agricultural issues, partly to reduce local dependence on the extension staff hired by the project. The KRIBHCO project, on the other hand, is hiring local people to be trained as facilitators: it is assumed they will, sometime in the future, take over the tasks presently being undertaken by the project staff. As Cromwell and Wiggins (1993) remarked, however, critical assessment of the feasibility of such strategies and plans are rare. This, they argue, is due to the lack of awareness of the institutional role the projects fill, often replacing, supplementing or providing alternatives to existing institutions. Others note that such plans must face up to very pragmatic issues, such as potential job losses, which are quite independent of the participatory process.

The question of sustainability is also related to the practice of group formation: should new groups be formed or new activities be implemented through existing groups? In addition to the earlier references to this issue, Loevinsohn et al., (1993) have argued that self-structured groups with demonstrated cohesion and regular contact, possibly for reasons other than crop cultivation, make more persistent and dynamic research partners than those whose members have only a limited ongoing relationship (for example where they are selected by researchers). However, the seed study by Cromwell and Wiggins (1993) concluded that few non-governmental organizations are using:

> existing community structures and working with local varieties or adapted modern varieties appropriate to small farmers' needs... Most instead set up new local seed multiplication and distribution systems and work with modern varieties produced by formal sector agricultural research. This has serious implications for the long-run sustainability of the local seed systems supported by NGOs, which over-ride NGOs' expressed aims of empowerment, community control and responding to felt needs (p.99).

At the same time there are programmes which have noted the fact that new people come forward when new groups are formed. Thus in the ICIPE programme, an analysis of the leadership of 26 local groups demonstrated that the same people were involved in almost all the groups. The research team concluded that while new groups potentially allow new people to come forward, in order for this to happen, support from outsiders may be needed.[5]

Sperling (1992), while not actually involved in a development programme, raised other questions about the sustainability of introduced activities, and in particular the 'professionalizing' of the women bean experts with whom the Rwanda programme was working. The risk is of turning these women into adjuncts of the formal research programme and thus isolating them from their families, communities and farms (the very source of their expertise). Van der Bliek and van Veldhuizen (1993) raise a somewhat different problem relating to the sustainability of organizations involved in the development of agricultural equipment: the need to involve groups or individuals who might eventually manufacture the new products. In a number of the programmes they reviewed this was not done and potential project sustainability was weakened.

An important aspect of the discussion relating to sustainability is how often do farmers actually need to change what they are doing? Can producers be continually testing new ideas and techniques? It is implied

---

[5] This whole discussion is related to an earlier debate about the evolutionary nature of technological and institutional change. Biggs (1984) comments that problems in the institutionalization process stem from a transfer rather than an evolutionary approach to the strengthening of local scientific capabilities. Clay (1984) takes up this same line of argument.

by the detailed analysis of Stassart and Mukandakasa (1992) that the process can be fairly continuous although they emphasize that the project does not necessarily see groups as permanent. The general lack of understanding of local processes of experimentation and innovation (are there normal 'cycles' of innovative behaviour? what are appropriate indicators of the health or sustainability of these processes?) means that most projects that seek to affect these are poorly placed to answer such questions.

Sustainable agriculture and agro-ecological approaches

From the material reviewed, it emerges clearly that farmer participatory research is being used both to test and disseminate existing technologies (which may or may not already be present in the programme areas), and to develop new technology. As discussed in earlier chapters, farmer participatory research is closely associated with the call for an alternative technological agenda appropriate for small farmers living in diverse, often marginal environments.

Bebbington and Thiele (1993) referred to the particular case of CAAP in Ecuador, which is working with the Andean peasants to build technology based on their own production rationales, characterized by long-term ecosystem conservation, domestic, ritual and social food production needs and optimum use of available labour. In general, however, they concluded from their review that the NGOs operating in Latin and Central America experience problems in trying to work within these bounds. They identified the critical issue as the initial fall in production and income that is often associated with the introduction of agro-ecological strategies.[6] Many NGOs therefore, like national research systems, begin with simple, high pay-off technologies. More generally they noted that 'many NGOs see a key role for modern technologies and mechanization in solving problems of colonist farming.'

Bebbington and Thiele (1993) suggest that even if there are technical successes, problems with the agro-ecological approach may persist in the long-term, because of the lack of markets for the products of such systems.[7] Others are cautious for different reasons. Posner and Gilbert (1991), for example, refer to the complexity of the agro-ecological approach itself. They examined the current emphasis on sustainable

---

[6] Some argue strongly that individual crop productivity may well fall but overall 'system output' is likely to increase, especially in high rainfall areas (D. Gibbon, personal communication).

[7] They do refer to the special case of organic cocoa production by El Ceibo, Bolivia, which was able to profit from the high market price facilitated by European fair-trade NGOs.

80

agriculture within the context of what they have referred to as 'the unique ecology of semi-arid West Africa', and concluded that the exercise demonstrated the complexity of the task and the dearth of solutions available. They argued that in the next ten years there will be relatively few good matches between actual production objectives of farmers and available sustainable agriculture technologies: available technologies tend to be labour intensive or involve draught animal power, neither of which appear interesting for the West African semi-arid zone. Finally, they suggested that the shift in focus to sustainable agriculture themes can be seen as a shift away from the farmers' agenda, which is to raise net incomes through increased production and/or reduced unit costs. Although ICLARM researchers are amongst the strongest supporters of these approaches among the CGIAR institutes, they would appear to concur with Posner and Gilbert – farmers will only be partners in conservation when it is profitable (Lightfoot and Pullin, 1991). These authors are also concerned to point out that special arrangements (i.e., subsidies) may be necessary to support long-term conservation.

The issue might, however, be even more complex. As already discussed, a number of NGOs in Latin America are using the sustainable agriculture theme as part of a broader effort to define a separate identity (i.e., the modernist versus indigenous knowledge dichotomy), while seeking a radically different technical agenda (as opposed to the development of new technology). As Bebbington and Thiele (1993) point out, these organizations are faced with the dilemma of farmer knowledge having often incorporated 'modern technologies' which the NGOs find hard to incorporate into their agro-ecological approaches. Hence, they observed a tendency for NGOs to focus only on knowledge and local information they want to hear. Lightfoot et al. (1993), amongst others, warn against too much romanticizing about traditional farming:

> farmers know a lot, but they do not know everything. Many processes which threaten the quality of agricultural resources cannot be observed with the naked eye and farmers know little of tomorrow's world and future technologies.

They state emphatically that sustainable systems cannot simply be constructed by going back to traditional farming systems which collapsed under intensification and resource extraction. Some external inputs will be necessary to produce sustainable systems. These views are shared by others (van Keulen and Breman, 1990).

Nevertheless, some successes have been reported. For example, the development of low input systems integrating aquaculture and crop production in Malawi, Ghana and Bangladesh was reported in Chapter 4. Within these systems, wastes are reused and pollutants kept to a minimum, and '...household cash income and food supply can be significantly increased if farmers' resource management skills are improved using mapping and modelling techniques combined with exposure to different systems illustrating possibilities for integration and recycling of farm resources' (Lightfoot and Noble, 1992). However, it is early to talk of the long-term success of these systems (Lightfoot *et al.*, 1992), and there are some experiences with similar systems which have not been successful due to various technical and economic factors (e.g., Cruz *et al.*, 1992).

Despite the comment by Bebbington and Thiele (1993) that NGOs working in Latin and Central America frequently take a 'modernist approach' to technology development and, in general, do not engage in the promotion of new products, they also report that agro-ecological themes, in particular agro-forestry and integrated pest management, are rapidly gaining in popularity. Wellard and Copestake (1993) note the massive increase in forestry and agro-forestry development (not usually research) programmes in Africa since the droughts of the 1970s and 1980s, with NGOs playing a major role in community forestry programmes. However, as they point out, these programmes have been supported by large quantities of external funds. Almost all national and international research systems, not only those in Africa, now have some research on agroforestry.

Whose research agenda?

We noted in our introductory chapter that farmer participatory research is part of a development agenda which is concerned with changing the orientation of formal research.[8] Thus Gubbels (1992b), amongst others, argues that while teaching farmers about scientific experimentation will increase their demand pull on research, effective strategies must address the broader structural issues. We also raised the question of whether farmer participatory research programmes will necessarily be any better placed than farming systems research or other research approaches to deal

---

[8] Much of the literature presumes that the interface is always between farmers on the one hand and national research or extension systems on the other. However, a number of non-government organizations involved in farmer participatory research of one kind or another face similar problems with their research agendas. Specifically, Bebbington and Thiele (1993) note that 'Actual participation is weaker than the rhetoric suggests. Most decisions are still made by NGO managers and donors.' In the same volume, competition and conflict about who is setting the agenda also arise between non-government organizations and farmers' organizations (and other 'membership' organizations).

with larger policy issues[9]. As was pointed out in earlier chapters, the discussion of the empowerment of clients and 'democratization' of research can be addressed at different levels: individual communities, individual researchers, research institutes, etc. At the more macro-level, change frequently takes a long time, and is thus particularly difficult to achieve within most project time-frames. The fact that the majority of projects are geographically distant from decision-making centres and work at the level of communities, individual farmers and individual researchers is another factor constraining potential impact at the macro-level. In this respect, farmer participatory research again appears to be in a position similar to farming systems research.

Didier (1993), for example, has pointed to the fact that proponents of farming systems research continue to highlight processes at the level of farms (some go no further than looking at decision-making surrounding activities such as trials) rather than processes by which policy decision-makers might be influenced. The potential impact of farmer participatory research activities on policy issues is partly related to the nature of the links between different interest groups within the research community: scientists and technicians, on-station and on-farm, strategic and applied. Again, the problem is not specific to farmer participatory research, but is common to client-led research as a whole. The question is, can research clients (and client-led research in the broadest sense) drive the rest of the research system?

There are many examples of the complexity of the problem. Biggs (1989) detailed the case of the national agricultural research system in Ecuador. Both field agronomists and technicians work from physically isolated regional stations, and for various other reasons (e.g., they are young and have little experience) find it difficult to defend their projects in the face of criticism from more experienced scientists. This case contrasts starkly with examples Biggs provides from India where senior scientists were themselves engaged in on-farm research. This made it possible for them to change the existing allocations of research personnel and other resources between on-farm and on station activities (Biggs, 1983; 1984). Drinkwater (1992), in describing the Zambia adaptive research teams, goes even further. While referring to problems of linkage between commodity-oriented scientists and others, he also notes the specialization within the teams themselves, with social scientists being specifically designated to 'talk to farmers'. He suggests that the teams have not really been 'engaged' enough to get beyond the conventional relations between research, extension and farmers. Biggs and Pound

---

[9] Biggs and Clay (1981) list some of the research policy issues specific to agricultural technology development: genetic vulnerability, choices between environmentally specific or widely adapted technology, the location of research activity and the links between agricultural producers and scientists.

(1992) suggest guidelines for strengthening the links between station and on-farm research and identify conditions where farmer participatory (and presumably all client-led) research might be expected to be more productive. Some of the these conditions include the situation where there are actual agreements between scientists on their respective roles, where the scientific credibility of on-farm research is high, and where the personal costs and benefits of on-farm research are acknowledged.

How have farmer participatory research programmes been implementing strategies to affect policy change? Again, both direct and indirect approaches have been taken. Various programmes, including FarmLink and the Food Security Project at Chivi, are working towards changing individual researchers through their link programmes (an indirect approach). Biggs and Pound (1992) suggest that the publications and advocacy role of Farm Africa in Ethiopia is also contributing to changes in policy. We have already referred to a number of similar programmes which are assembling material on producer systems for which formal research systems have little if any information. Apart from these specific cases, however, all farmer participatory research programmes are presumed to have some wider impact beyond the individual producer or community, in the short or long-term: by increasing awareness in clients of the existence of the formal research system. The majority of programmes are at the same time addressing this issue through organizing their clients, on the premise that better organized farmers have more political and financial power. Others have concentrated on the possibility of existing organizations acting as brokers on behalf of local groups (SAVE, for example). A number of writers would agree with Gubbels (1992a), however, that unless the question is addressed directly at the level of planning committees and institutions as a whole, no sustainable change in policy can be achieved.

There has been a concerted effort by a number of government institutions to change their modes of behaviour, often at the instigation of donors. ISNAR has played a key role in defining strategies to enhance more participatory decision-making institutions (see Bingen and Poats, 1990). Merrill-Sands and Kaimowitz (1990) list seven conditions for an effective partnership with clients which are expected to result in reversals of management problems and end in empowerment. These include creating opportunities for interaction; seeking agreement on tasks; cultivating mutual respect; shared goals; promoting an understanding of interdependence; mutual perception as partners not competitors; personal benefits outweighing costs. Some of these conditions echo the concept of the collegiate mode of interaction (and the conditions for linking station-based and field-based researchers referred to earlier) and as we have observed, advances in creating appropriate settings for dialogue along these lines have been made and shifts from contractual to collaborative modes of interaction have been reported for a number of farming systems programmes. ATIP in Botswana is a frequently cited example but others were reported at the 12th Annual FSR/E symposium (e.g., Rajasekaran [1992] for India and Kar *et al.* [1992] for Bangledesh). The adaptive farming systems research teams in Zambia have, within the last three years, switched to a predominantly collaborative mode after ten years (Drinkwater, 1992). These teams now collaborate with village research groups. Similar progress has been reported for the Zairian National Legume Programme at Mulungu where the researchers have consciously looked at farmers' own experimentation to help evaluate their own trial designs. They are also trying to work with communities rather than individuals, especially with women's co-operatives (CIAT, 1992). Bebbington and Thiele (1993) observed changes within some national research programmes within Latin American in response to criticism. Fujisaka (1992) described IRRI's breeding programmes as 'eliciting and applying farmers' technical knowledge associated with germplasm'. Farmer knowledge and rice seed is collected to better conserve and utilize rice bio-diversity[10]. Nevertheless, most of these changes do not reflect increased demand pull of rural clients even though Fujisaka suggests that farmers could be involved in the identification of the research problem (Fujisaka, 1989).

Some organizations have commissioned or plan to commission research from the formal system on behalf of their clients. A union of cassava producers in Ecuador, UAPPI, uses USAID funds to contract research from the university and public sector. The Farm Africa project described in Chapter 4 plans to contract research from formal research organizations (Farm Africa, 1993). Ashby (1992) even argued that if farmers themselves can contract research, they will be able to penalize researchers who make mistakes. Such a situation would be dependent on the existence of well-organized farmer groups, which in turn depend on effective leader–constituency exchange relationships and the ability to diagnose and prioritize research needs.

The more common response to the problem of poor linkages is increased client representation on research planning committees.[11] As Biggs (1989) points out, resource-rich farmers often participate in meetings at research stations and have associations which lobby for

---

[10] However, at a broader level, Fujisaka (1992) predicted a decline in the level of farmer participation following the CGIAR Technical Advisory Committee's recommendation that the CGIAR centres should focus on 'basic' and 'strategic' research activities while increasing collaboration with national institutions which would conduct 'applied' and 'adaptive' research.

[11] Waibel and Beaden (1990) report on a programme which brought farmers into farming systems research teams as 'specialist consultants'.

research. Regional committees comprized of researchers, administrators and farmers are part of the decentralized structures being promoted by the World Bank. In Chile, farmers are on the committees of the different Centres for Adaptation and Transfer of Technology (CATT). Merrill-Sands and Collion (1992) have proposed that non-governmental organizations can represent resource poor farmers. The efficacy of this approach depends partly on the extent to which these organizations have already cut themselves off from the formal system, a problem raised particularly by Bebbington and Thiele (1993) in relation to NGOs in Latin America. Of course, as noted earlier, a few NGOs also employ their own research staff, thus avoiding the problem of linking with the formal system. However, the problem of shifting the control of the research agenda toward the clients may still remain.

Merrill-Sands and Collion (1992), reflecting an increasing level of frustration, have also suggested that what is needed is a repackaging of existing information (derived from farming systems research) specifically for policy-makers. They ask: 'How can qualitative data be packaged?' The problem as far as they are concerned extends to the location specificity of much of the research which leads to 'intermittent and unco-ordinated feedback' which is not suitable for sound decision-making on research priorities. They have argued that the optimum solution is to organize a basic data set covering all regions.

There are also issues which are beyond farmer participatory research in the sense being discussed here. Farrington and Bebbington (1993) identified some factors about which research managers can do little, such as the policy and political contexts of agricultural research including donor agendas, institutional mandates, commodity programme priorities and national development goals, all of which affect research agendas. As we have already observed, these affect all types of organizations.

A number of writers question the level and type of impact which clients might be expected to have on research. Thus some argue that most research is not completed within a single production cycle whereas farmers' articulated demands are frequently seen as relating to short-run priorities. Baker (1992) has suggested that this is particularly problematic when options for sustainable systems are on the agenda since these usually involve long-term research programmes. Haugerud and Collinson (1990) have observed that even plant breeders cannot 'respond to every quirk of farmers' circumstances but the relevance of breeding research in poor nations can be improved.' Zadek (1993) has argued that formal research will continue to take the lead because '...in practice, it is almost impossible not to allow the weight of history to privilege a particular perspective.'

Finally there is the wider issue of the relationship between government institutions and rural people: 'participatory research has no genuine currency in the absence of a decentralization of power on a scale which remains a remote possibility in many states' (Gatter, 1993:182, referring to Africa).

Information needs prior to implementation

The literature indicates at least four key areas which must inform the design and orientation of farmer participatory research activities: farmer experimentation; institutions and patterns of social and economic relations; flows of resources and information; and knowledge gaps. The participatory diagnostic exercises based on PRA techniques that are now being carried out within most programmes prior to implementation are designed to provide a holistic view of land use and livelihoods. However, they do not generally, and perhaps cannot provide detailed information on what often are complex issues and processes. We will argue in a later section that the lack of knowledge about these on-going processes may be one reason why significant gaps between theory and practice of farmer participatory research are apparent, and in particular why programmes look so similar when the theory would indicate that diversity of strategies and activities should be the rule.

It can be argued that a thorough understanding of farmers' logic and methods of experimentation, and the local perception of the value of farmers' experimentation ('whether it is progressive and possesses development potential' [Richards, 1992]), must be at the centre of all farmer participatory research programmes. Nevertheless, it appears that few projects actually study these processes.[12] The Farm Africa project in Ethiopia attempted to identify farmers' own research but was unsuccessful – it was unable to identify innovative farmers in the project area or varieties or techniques other than those introduced by the national research system (Farm Africa, 1992).[13] A number of programmes which work with people defined as 'experimenters' (FarmLink and SAVE) and 'experts' (Sperling et al., 1993), have been noted, but in general definitions and selection criteria are vague. While typologies of farmer experiments have been proposed (Rhodes and Bebbington, 1991), others have suggested that in fact is is impossible to distinguish farmers' experimental activities from the production process itself (Stolzenbach, 1992a).

---

[12] Some project field staff may have acquired a considerable understanding of local processes, but this information does not appear to be accessible to planners or other project staff.

[13] It should be noted in conjunction with this report that the communities are made up of settled immigrants and there has been a significant level of disorganization within them over the last twenty years.

As yet, no generally accepted view of the nature of farmers' own experimentation has emerged. Richards (1992) suggests that farmers have validation procedures similar to formal science, including replication and peer review. However, according to Richards the main issue is whether or not farmers have the ability to develop significant new understanding under changing conditions. It is precisely this ability that determines if local knowledge is progressive and has development potential.

Much of the discussion of farmer experimentation takes place at the level of individual decision-making units while many programmes are operating at the level of groups and whole communities. Decisions to work with whole communities would seem to demand information on community systems of problem-solving and information exchange. Again, as appears to be the case with local experimentation, most projects seem to devote relatively few resources to understanding these issues, yet group formation and institution-building activities are at the core of many programmes. As indicated previously, where baseline studies of groups have been made, these have informed decisions about whether to create new groups or build on existing ones. It is nevertheless a complex issue of social reorganization which partly depends on local patterns of social and economic relations. In describing contemporary efforts to develop participatory irrigation tank management in Tamil Nadu, Mosse (1992) points to the need for longitudinal studies to examine tank irrigation systems as they operated in the past, factors associated with their degradation during the present century and changes in village social and political relations. This information would provide a context for a comparative study of present day efforts to re-establish local organizations for the rehabilitation of community irrigation systems.

A number of aspects which must be considered in institution building are listed in KRIBHCO (1992), including local attitudes to association for secular purposes; the choice of a starting point for an association for secular purposes; the level at which groups should be formed; group size and relation to existing social solidarities; the nature of leadership, etc. Clearly group processes are far from uniform, either in phasing or in the nature of the institutions which emerge. The KRIBHCO report indicates that many social variables are likely to affect the process, including settlement pattern, degree of social heterogeneity, social stratification or factionalism and extent of seasonal migration. Gender analysis and planning for women's involvement introduce additional complexities. Finally, local institutions are built within an existing set of social relationships: it is not simply a question of replacing and/or competing with existing systems but also interacting with them (also see Biggs, 1984) .

The earlier work of Horton (1981) and the more recent studies by Cromwell and Wiggins (1993) on the distribution of planting material within communities, illustrate the potential importance of an understanding of processes by which resources, including information, flow. From a series of case studies they described a complex system of seed procurement through which farmers obtain a range of crops and varieties from different sources at different times. On this basis, they question some projects' simplistic assumptions about seed sharing and thus the distribution of potential benefits from seed programmes.[14]

Finally, on the issue of knowledge diffusion, Bebbington (1990) has indicated that in order to understand how knowledge is communicated amongst peasant farmers one needs to consider what is communicated, how it is responded to, the relations of power, the affinity between the agents involved and the wider social and historical origins of these relationships. It should be clear from all the points raised that considerable skills in social analysis will be required.

Studies of the knowledge base and knowledge gaps within rural communities are probably amongst some of the more detailed and there are examples of such studies having been used to focus programme activities. Bentley (1993) describes how the Panamerican Agricultural School deals with the 'important but difficult to observe' category of farmer knowledge which, he argues, is especially challenging to address in a collaborative manner (Table 5.3). Thus, in the school's pest management programme, the emphasis is on two things that farmers do not generally know: how insects reproduce and what kills the insects. According to Bentley, the research agronomists concentrate on enhancing farmers' knowledge rather than on telling them how to do experiments. Thus, the programme is based on the premise that effective technical collaboration with farmers necessitates:

learning what rural people know and what they don't, figuring out what they need to know, teaching it to them in a way consistent with what they know, and then learning from them as they synthesize new information with old knowledge.

---

[14] Traditional seed diffusion mechanisms are often well established, elaborate structures based on and developing out of the traditional channels of exchange. However, Cromwell and Wiggins (1993) concluded that there is no evidence that individual farmers set themselves up permanently as large-scale seed producers for sale within the local community. Rather it appears that individuals, who may change from year to year, are approached by other members of the community because they are seen to have a good stand of crops growing or they have planted a new variety which appears to be performing well. The exception to this is where individuals with some kind of traditional status within the community are approached by poorer households reflecting patterns of traditional obligations or patronage. Nevertheless, some seed diffusers also display a 'personal commitment and interest in promoting development in their community... they are not simply the richer farmers or those who have access to new varieties first' (p.31).

Table 5.3 Characterisation of farmer knowledge by importance and ease of observation

Importance	Ease of observation	
	[–]	[+]
+	- Many catagories - Shallow taxonomy - Organisms labelled at biological order or family level - Little explanation	- Many catagories - Multi-layered taxonomy - Organisms labelled at biological species level - 'Positivist' explanation
–	- No catagories - No taxonomy - No organisms labelled - No explanation	- Sometimes many catagories - Sometimes shallow taxonomy - Some organisms labelled at biological species level - Explanations from folklore

Source: Bentley (1991)

Bentley and Andrews (1991) conclude that from an ethno-science perspective, it is important to study topics where farmer knowledge is less encyclopedic, and to explain gaps in peoples' knowledge. They suggest that pests and diseases, for example, are subjects about which farmers appear to have limited knowledge (also see Richards, 1978; ActionAid–Uganda/NRI, 1992; Bentley, 1992b; ICIPE, 1992, 1993; Riches and Saxton, 1993).

The question of appropriate modes of intervention when farmers have little previous knowledge about a new crop or a problem has also been raised. This was a central concern of George *et al.* (1992) in their evaluation of the SAVE project. They argued that extension staff should give additional information or recommendations to farmers when the crop or varieties being distributed are not familiar to the recipients. This suggestion runs counter to the project strategy of simply feeding raw material into an on-going process of experimentation and innovation through the distribution of small quantities of planting material. Clearly, when a new crop or process is under consideration, clients may need more information. The issue would appear to be, however, how far to go with prescribing limits and possibilities in order not to restrict choice or options. Some of the more intense discussions among ActionAid/NRI field staff have revolved around this very issue of the appropriate type of intervention when farmer information or experience is limited (A. Martin, personal communication), and similar concerns have arisen at ITDG (S. Croxton, personal communication). This question was also considered in the report by van der Bliek and van Veldhuizen (1993) on the role of participation in the development of tools, equipment and techniques in appropriate technology programmes. Biggs and Pound (1992), with reference to the Farm Africa project in Ethiopia, noted that researchers designed an alley farming trial because farmers knew nothing about the subject. The trial was subsequently to be used to generate discussions about trial layout and management modification to suit farmer circumstances.

At the same time as knowledge gaps are being highlighted, as indicated in Chapter 4, programmes are pulling together local knowledge on various subjects, including subjects about which there is little published information. Farm Africa in Ethiopia has been particular active in this area (Adebo, 1992; Alemu and Sandford, 1991). In some cases techniques or varieties are subsequently tested prior to dissemination. One of the earlier examples of this is reported by Macdonald and Bartlett (1985) in Pakistan: innovations were screened and tested in on-farm trials to establish their suitability for the majority of farmers, and only subsequently disseminated through extension.

With a note of caution, Bentley and Andrews (1991) point out that most small-scale farmers are in transition and their practices disrupted, which makes such studies even more vital. But at the same time it is important to avoid a romantic or sentimental view of traditional farmers. Richards (1992) warns that it is essential to distinguish between different kinds of local knowledge since it is not all useful for rural development. He asks, 'What is the relevant local knowledge.' Presumably, in most instances it refers to skills and understanding adapted to the peculiarities of the local agro-climatic and socio-economic environment. Mosse (1993) indicates that local knowledge which is still under discussion or is disputed is generally not available to outsiders. If true, this is unfortunate since it is precisely this information which might provide the most useful guidelines as to possible areas of collaboration.

Conclusion

Chapters 4 and 5 have provided an overview of recent experiences with the implementation of farmer participatory research. One point is clear: what began as a relatively simple call for more involvement of clients in agricultural research has become a complex web of theoretical and practical issues. So far, we have suggested that there are two basic approaches that have been used in the implementation of farmer participatory research, and we have described these as more and less interventionist. We have also suggested that these approaches have implications for the sustainability of programmes. Apart from this distinction, there is a remarkable level of similarity in practices and associated issues between different farmer participatory research projects. Thus, most projects place considerable emphasis on participative diagnosis of problems, on-farm trials and group approaches to development. It is probably with respect to the group or community orientation that farmer participatory research can be differentiated most clearly from farming systems research.

It would appear from the examples that farmer participatory research, as it is presently being implemented, can be expensive especially in terms of the time commitment of both researchers and clients, and in some instances it requires specialist skills for success. From the point of view of researchers (who are generally few in number), hard questions need to be asked about what kinds of research, what methods, approaches and activities are most productive for achieving specific results. At the same time, farmers who agree to work with researchers need to see results. Baker (1991), for example, is convinced that what farmers need are new options and that they are not seeking catalysts to their own innovative processes.

Considerable attention is still being given to the promotion and use of PRA techniques and tools because of their ease of use and the perception that they provide an effective way to move towards greater participation. They are now widely used for carrying out diagnostic work but are also used in the evaluation of on-farm trials. Meanwhile, concerns are being expressed, as was the case with farming systems research, about the lack of clear links between initial problem analysis and actual programme activities.

The chapter that follows, therefore, provides a critical evaluation of the examples presented in Chapters 4 and 5. The emphasis is on evidence of success in moving toward a more collegiate mode of interaction between farmers and researchers. At the same time, we return to some of the implementation issues discussed in this chapter. Special attention is given to the two major common activities: participative diagnosis and the use of PRA techniques and on-farm trials.

6 An Analysis of Current Trends and Practice

THIS CHAPTER BEGINS by relating the material presented in Chapters 4 and 5 to other types and forms of agricultural research, and assessing these in terms of the mode of interaction between researchers and farmers. This analysis stems from the earlier observation that one of the key objectives of farmer participatory research is to move towards a more collegiate relationship between researchers and farmers. The examples of on-going farmer participatory research provide an opportunity to evaluate progress along this front. The question of the non-financial costs and benefits (for both farmers and researchers) that have been attributed to farmer participatory research is then addressed. This issue is approached in two ways: firstly using the basic versus adaptive categorization of research, and secondly, through the stages in technology development, from notional to finished product. The discussion then turns to an in-depth analysis of the two most common 'participatory' activities, problem identification and on-farm trials. The chapter ends by returning to the question of the types of technology for which farmer participatory research may be particularly useful.

The movement towards participation

The overview begins with a broad assessment of how effective farmer participatory research has been in fostering closer integration of farmers' own research and the formal agricultural research system. In Chapters 4 and 5 we explored some examples of recent attempts to increase farmer participation in and interaction with formal research, and attention was drawn to attempts being made to reconcile the nature and characteristics of farmer experimentation with more formal research methods and perspectives. For the purpose of this analysis we will use the three stages of the research process introduced previously: identifying opportunities; identifying options; testing and adapting.

The examples provide clear evidence of extensive farmer involvement in activities to identify problems, opportunities and possible solutions. This has been facilitated in many programmes by the shift from long-term surveys (which became a central element of the practice though not necessarily the theory of farming systems research), to PRA techniques. There is also evidence of some increase in farmer participation in, and interaction with, on-station research. Perhaps the most common form of participation is in terms of farmer visits to the experiment stations. These visits are clearly related to traditional 'field days', during which farmers view experimental plots and demonstrations. In some cases, these visits are now meant to provide ideas for the farmers' own experimentation. The crop variety selection programmes discussed in Chapter 4 involve more active participation by farmers in station-based research. There are, however, few examples of farmers having a direct and active role in determining either the general orientation or the details of experiment station research.

A number of the farmer participatory research activities reviewed in Chapter 4 have established on-farm trial programmes, and these are usually discussed in terms of facilitating or enhancing farmers' experimentation. Many of these programmes involve, or are initiated with, training of farmers in experimental techniques (plot layout, replication, data collection, etc.). Thus, because of the level of training, intervention and control by project staff, these programmes closely resemble the 'farmer-managed trials' that represented the cutting edge of farmer participation within farming systems research. A few programmes have taken a more 'hands-off' approach to the farmers' own experimentation, providing little training or direction. There would seem, however, to be little systematic basis for the choice between the more or less interventionist strategies.

There are a few examples of researchers monitoring farmers' own experimentation, although this has clearly not emerged as a priority activity. The more common approach has been for programmes to encourage mutual monitoring by local farmers, rather than involving the researcher directly.

Thus, using the stages in the research process and the modes of participation discussed earlier, Figure 6.1 presents a summary of the scope and nature of the farmer participatory research activities (Frame 1). This representation must be seen in comparison to 'traditional' agricultural research (Frame 2), farming systems research (Frame 3) and farmers' own research (Frame 4). As introduced in Chapter 2, this framework acknowledges that researchers and farmers are also involved in independent (i.e., non-participative) research and activities, that may well incorporate ideas or options from other parts of the continuum.

To date, therefore, farmer participatory research appears to have put farmers at the forefront of diagnostic activities, while marginally strengthening their involvement in both on-station research and on-farm trials. As a result, there has been something of a shift from a contractual/consultative to a consultative/collaborative relationship. On the other hand, we would argue, there has not been significant progress in creating a 'collegiate interface' between more formal research and

94

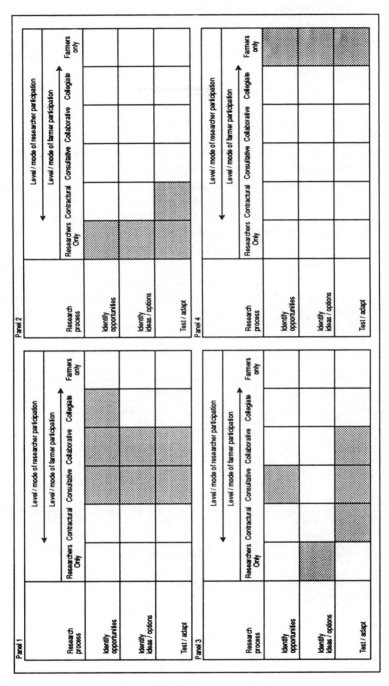

Figure 6.1 *Summary of the scope and nature of farmer participatory research activities presented in Chapters 4 and 5*

farmers' own experimental activities (as depicted, for example, in Figure 6.2). We believe that this apparent lack of progress reflects the fact that (i) much farmer participatory research is taking place within the context of farming systems research programmes, (ii) regardless of the wider institutional context, most programmes are still concerned with evaluating, adapting and extending technologies developed previously by the formal research system and (iii) despite the rhetoric and several pieces of much-cited literature, few programmes appear to have yet understood how to interact with farmers' own experimental interests and skills.

This leads to a consideration of where, within the whole spectrum of agricultural technology development and testing, farmer participatory research is now considered as having a major role to play. This question can be approached in terms of the perceived value of farmer participatory research to development organizations, researchers and farmers.[15] Rather, for the moment the concern is with farmers and researchers, regardless of their institutional affiliations. The assumption is neither that in order to be successful, agricultural research must necessarily involve *both* farmers and researchers, nor that farmer participatory approaches will be appropriate in all situations. Whether farmer participatory research is used or not clearly depends on a number of issues including the nature of the specific research problem, the inclination, or attitudes of the researchers,

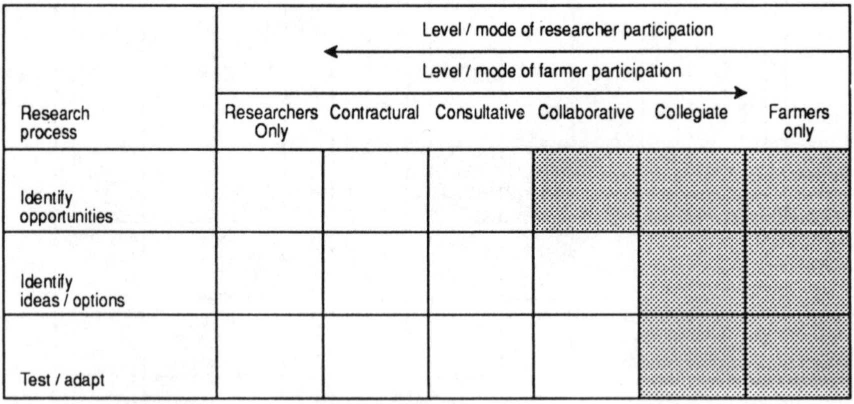

Research process	Researchers Only	Contractual	Consultative	Collaborative	Collegiate	Farmers only
	Level / mode of researcher participation ←					
	Level / mode of farmer participation →					
Identify opportunities				▓	▓	▓
Identify ideas / options					▓	▓
Test / adapt					▓	▓

Figure 6.2 *Scope and nature of a collegial interface between farmer participatory research and formal research*

---

[15] As indicated in Chapter 3 (also see Figure 3.1), the discussion of institutional comparative advantage is legitimized in large part by the separation of the research function into categories such as basic, strategic, applied and adaptive. We would argue, however, that there is a strong case for a much more flexible approach to the conception of research responsibilities and roles. Such an approach would begin with a particular research challenge, and only then consider possible institutional configurations.

the resources available and the degree of interest or skill which the community has in carrying out research. One can assume, however, that all agricultural research must be directed towards meeting the needs of some specified group of clients.

The discussion that follows also assumes that all potential participants in farmer participatory research have other things they need to do: farmers farm (and do many other things), and researchers have institutional and administrative obligations, prepare documentation, communicate with colleagues, etc., apart from undertaking research which does not directly involve client participation. As the most common initiators of collaboration, however, it is researchers who are responsible for creating the situation within which effective participatory research can take place: the burden of initiating and sustaining a dialogue rests with them (a situation which, Bentley [1990] concludes, can be both 'frustrating and unwieldy').

The niche of farmer participatory research

Cost is an important consideration in the literature on farmer participatory research just as it was for farming systems research. Many of the points raised with respect to the expense of farmer participatory research echo these earlier (and continuing) discussions.[16] Much of the debate concerning the cost of farming systems research referred specifically to situations where farming systems research teams and activities were added to existing research institutions, structures and programmes. They were generally not seen as replacements or substitutes for other models of research and indeed many efforts to institutionalize farming systems research involved the addition of new researchers. However, there is work that demonstrates that participative trials and programmes result in more productive (higher-yielding) technologies and greater project success (Ashby, 1987; Finsterbusch and van Wicklin, 1989). Reports of the results of integrating farmers into crop breeding programmes are equally positive: 'farmers have the edge over breeders in selecting for specific production niches; longer-term adoption rates of farmer-selected varieties are high' (CIAT, 1992 p.7).

There has been a more or less explicit assumption that increased levels of farmer participation will only be valuable in relation to specific stages of the technology development and testing process. Perhaps the most

---

[16] We note, however, that many farmer participatory research projects are implemented by NGOs in the context of time-bound projects without strong institutional linkages. The issue of the financial implications of institutionalization and sustainability are thus somewhat different than those encountered with much farming systems research taking place primarily in the context of government institutions, which will presumably outlive any individual project.

commonly used framework for the analysis of agricultural research distinguishes between the basic, strategic, and adaptive functions. While our particular concern is farmer participatory research, the debate about its potential contribution to the 'agricultural technology system' closely resembles the larger debate about on-farm research more generally.

Much has also been written about the appropriate location, either on-station or on-farm, for the different research functions. For example, Merrill-Sands and McAllister (1988) in their comparative analysis of nine national research systems viewed the applied research function (what they referred to as the 'technology generation function') as most appropriately located on-station. They argued that on-station research has a comparative advantage in terms of technology generation. On the other hand, on-farm research was seen principally as an activity for adjusting and adapting technology, functions which involve some level of site specificity and field diagnosis. Bebbington and Thiele (1993) in their discussion of the work of NGOs in Latin and Central America, break the process into two phases, selection and adjustment. Accordingly, technology selection implies evaluating the adaptation of technologies to an ecological zone, and frequently takes place on-station using experimental designs that can be analysed statistically. Technology adjustment involves the adaptation of the technologies to the socio-economic conditions of the farmer[17]. Some of ODI's recent studies go further than this, concluding that formal (station-based) research looks to generate technology which is then passed to intermediate users, including NGOs. In this scenario the formal elements of the research system, including national and international institutions, are involved in basic and applied research, while NGOs, with farmers, take major responsibility for adaptive research. Thus, as was true with much of the practice of farming systems research, the ODI case studies, and the more general analysis, highlight the adaptive end of the research continuum as the most appropriate sphere for farmer participation (see Figure 3.1).

As indicated in earlier chapters, the adaptive role that farmers can and do perform has long been recognized. In the more recent discussions of comparative advantage and appropriate actors vis-à-vis the continuum from basic to adaptive research, however, it is not entirely clear what farmers *themselves* would be (or are actually) doing, as against what they would be doing *with* researchers. In other words, what, if any, is the

---

[17] A range of other terms are used. In one report of the Small Ruminant CRSP programme the term 'experimentation' is used to refer to the testing of untried solutions to technological problems (preferably on-station) whereas the term 'validation' refers to local testing of technology already proven effective under similar agro-ecological conditions (McCorkle, 1990).

independent role of the farmers?

Much of the literature addresses what is seen to be a critical problem: the feedback of results between the different research functions, which are usually carried out in different locations and by different researchers. The concern with 'research–extension liaison' is one aspect of this issue. It is certainly true that at the level of many field personnel there is little distinction between an extension 'demonstration' and a research 'on-farm trial', and in many situations extension organizations have played a central role in implementing and monitoring on-farm research activities. Nevertheless, Merrill-Sands and McAllister (1988) concluded that the feedback function of on-farm research is performed poorly. They also found that the service function – the broad-scale, on-farm screening of technologies developed on-station – is also generally wanting.[18]

There are those who argued that farmers do have a role to play in both applied and strategic research, particularly for addressing such complex and difficult issues as weed management, soil fertility and 'natural resource management' (although in the case of the latter, it has been suggested that 'they may have barely perceived the problems' [Tripp, 1993]). Van der Bliek and van Veldhuizen (1993) provide four possible scenarios for farmer participation in the development of tools, equipment and techniques: (i) trying out what is coming from elsewhere, (ii) adapting what is coming from elsewhere according to local criteria, (iii) improving what already exists in the area and (iv) developing new tools. Biggs and Pound (1992) in their review of the Farm Africa Project in Ethiopia suggest that one of the main differences between a conventional farming systems research programme and the Farm Africa trials is the inclusion of farmers in technology development: earlier on-farm research programmes limited farmers' input to problem diagnosis and technology verification.

In Chapter 5 examples were given of farmers coming onto experiment stations, not simply to observe what was being done and identify potentially interesting information for themselves, but also to actually take part in the research (also see Haugerud and Collinson, 1990; Thapa *et al.*, 1992; Sperling *et al.*, 1993). Sperling *et al.* detailed the advantages

---

[18] It is interesting to find similar problems being discussed in the business world. In a recent discussion of the Palo Alto Research Center (PARC) set up by Xerox in the heart of the Silicon Valley as a centre for researchers to pursue new ideas, the following conclusions were reached: 'Most now agree that technology transfer – moving ideas from laboratory to workshop – is an oxymoron. Real know-how is embodied not in patents, research reports and prototypes but in the people who developed the idea. The one time that an innovation ... broke free from PARC and became a multi-billion dollar business for Xerox, it was because a 'champion' in the laboratory moved with it and drove the commercialization hard... The people at PARC were treated like inmates of a zoo – admired and fed but rarely let loose' (The Economist, July 10th 1993:92).

for plant breeders of bringing farmers to research stations, including farmers having earlier access to genetic material (which helps preserve diversity); the earlier identification of promising varieties (which saves time); larger number of varieties are selected (less wastage); and better adapted varieties are identified which are relatively high yielding on-farm (increasing technical efficiency). Their experience also indicates that farmers are aware of genotype-by-environment interaction and can predict this, with some accuracy, on-station. All their evidence suggests that this approach to participatory research yields better and faster results (and is less expensive) than more traditional breeding strategies combined with on-farm trials.

A framework proposed by Anderson and Hardaker (1979), which distinguishes between three categories of new and existing technology (notional, preliminary and developed), provides further support for the early involvement of farmers (Table 6.1). Menz and Knipscheer (1981) used this framework to discuss research costs. Their analysis revolves around the costs of evaluation which are associated with each stage of technology development (evaluation which, presumably, must be concluded before a technology moves to the next stage). In general, as technology development proceeds, more formalized (and costly) evaluation techniques are warranted. They conclude therefore, that 'on-farm experiments may become too costly because of logistical problems and locations become more specific which requires evaluations to be done in many locations.'

This question of location specificity and on-farm research features prominently in the farming systems research literature. The problem may be even greater with much farmer participatory research because of the concentration in highly variable agro-ecosystems. Thus Fujisaka *et al.* (1993b) have emphasized the need to examine recommendation domains in detail since small differences between groups of potential recipients can make a technology non-viable: specific technologies have very narrow niches. Menz and Knipscheer suggest that a potential method of minimizing the problem of location specificity is for research institutions to place a greater emphasis on the testing of 'preliminary' technologies. Under these circumstances, the general objective of formal research would be to maximize the probability of 'new discoveries' at the farm level. They agree with Anthony *et al.* (1979), who pose the question: 'Is it desirable that any research organization attempts to test and adapt a system to local farmer needs?' since this is an activity in which farmers already engage.

A number of authors have also observed that researchers are not, in any case, in a position to develop all the different technologies that farmers need (Andrews and Bentley, 1990; Sumberg and Okali, 1988; Biggs and Clay, 1981). Menz and Knipscheer (1981) add that the

Table 6.1 Framework for depicting stages of technology design and evaluation methods

Stages of technology design	Most cost-effective evaluation method
Notional	- Intuitional
	- Informal duscussions
	- Formalised discussions
Preliminary	- Laboratory experiments
	- Research station field experiments
	- Budgeting
Development	- Computer simulation experiments
	- Unit farms experiments
	- Researcher-managed on-farm trials
	- Farmer-managed on-farm trials

Adapted from Anderson and Hardaker (1979)

adaptation of technology is not an 'once only' process. Climate, disease, price and institutional changes all cause farmers to constantly adjust their farming systems and thus to modify their techniques. They conclude, therefore, that too much fine tuning of farming systems by researchers is not only expensive but also inappropriate.

Another approach which has been suggested is in terms of areas of knowledge. As indicated in Chapter 5, some practitioners work with farmers only on what can be defined as new areas of knowledge (see Bentley, [1991] and the ActionAid/Uganda example).

Participatory problem analysis

Participatory diagnostic activities are a part of most programmes of client-oriented research and development. They can be seen as a logical extension of the earlier interest in 'needs assessment', and are now commonly used to identify and prioritize areas for project intervention. The ubiquity of participatory diagnostic activities reflects, in large part, the popularization of RRA and PRA. There are now many national, regional and international institutions, and hundreds of individuals, heavily involved in promoting these approaches and their associated techniques and tools. The current fervour for RRA and PRA is, therefore, the appropriate backdrop for a discussion of the broader topic of participatory problem analysis as a component of farmer participatory research.

In many ways the detailed economic and technical baseline surveys that became established as part of the accepted practice of farming systems research were also its Achilles heel. These studies were supposed to identify major constraints to increased production and productivity, and were thus the logical first step in the research process. Unfortunately the scale, intensity and long-term nature of many of these surveys meant that results were rarely available as an input to research planning or programme development. While there was clearly a certain level of farmer participation, they have been broadly criticized as 'extractive', and some have suggested that they served only to validate a pre-set agenda.

Certainly the use of PRA techniques and tools within farmer participatory research projects has resulted in timely, descriptive reports which have tended to replace these time-consuming baseline studies. There is also fairly widespread agreement as to their value for this purpose.[19] While in some respects these do resemble earlier farming systems studies, more reference is made to local knowledge and perceptions. Gender specific issues and the difference between the knowledge of men and women are also highlighted. Nevertheless, while the amount of data generated by PRA techniques is smaller in comparison to formal surveys, information management remains a problem. A group of four to five people working for five days using PRA tools can produce a set of interesting information, much of it qualitative in nature, the analysis and presentation of which can present considerable problems. Pottier (1991) suggests that its interpretation depends upon detailed knowledge of socio-political contexts, and Merrill-Sands and Collion (1992) identify the problem of 'packaging' qualitative data.

Diagnostic exercises carried out by the farmer participatory research projects discussed in Chapter 4 have used the whole range of PRA tools, from mapping and transects to ranking and meetings. However, organized meetings, seminars and workshops are some of the more commonly used tools for participatory diagnosis. Five of the examples presented in Chapter 4 (Participatory Research and Extension Project, Rwanda; Chivi Food Security Project; The Agricultural Technology Improvement Programme, Botswana; Crop-Fish Systems Research; CID FarmLink Project) use meetings and workshops as an integral part of both problem diagnosis and programme development and evaluation. Within the FarmLink project, decisions are taken through a series of participatory workshops which begin with a general protocol meeting and end with an 'Innovation Analysis Workshop' and farm visits. They are also used as part of the process for identifying participants. Other examples can be found: Ravnborg (1992) described the 'Future workshop' evolved in Germany as a method for exploring possible alternative development

---

[19] A number of such descriptive reports using PRA tools within farming systems research programmes were presented at the 12th Annual FSR/E Symposium held in November 1992 (e.g., Timsina and Poudel, 1992; Tulachan and Batsa, 1992; Balakrishnan and Nyirahabimana, 1992). Others have been published by IIED (see for example Scoones and McCracken, 1989), and IDS in *RRA Notes*, while countless other RRA and PRA exercises remain as internal project documents.

paths, while Abedin and Haque (1987) referred to 'Innovator Farmer Workshops' in Bangladesh as a method of gaining information and insight into farmers' informal innovations and defining new research areas. The widely publicized 'group trek' in Nepal (Mathema and Galt, 1986; Bell and Garrod, 1986) is essentially a series of workshops, while Loevinsohn *et al.* (1993) in Rwanda used the term 'travelling seminars' to refer to meetings of groups from different locations to allow more thorough comparisons of available options.

In his review of nine national on-farm research programmes, Biggs (1989) identified two objectives for meetings: as a research tool for assembling, analysing and giving information, and as a means of organizing and managing farmer participation more efficiently and effectively. But as Mosse (1993) pointed out, the successful use of meetings as a participatory tool depends upon established links between an agency and local communities: appraisals do not take place in a historical, political, institutional and cultural vacuum, and all these factors will determine the outcome. The first response of communities to such participatory appraisals is usually based on recent experience with other outsiders (e.g., Hoffmann, 1990). In situations where there is a deeply entrenched suspicion of the motivation of outsiders, participatory styles of interaction are of little value. Reference to land issues in particular can raise anxieties. And finally, information generated by a PRA is influenced by the 'perceived' relationship between the informants and project staff which is itself rooted in expectations of the project.

As described in Chapter 4, ICLARM, based very much on the earlier work of Conway (1986), specializes in the development of 'systems science diagrams' to examine the transformation of degraded agro-ecosystems, and has produced a training resource book promoting their use (Lightfoot *et al.*, 1991). Along similar lines, Lightfoot and Pullin (1991) detailed how transects across agro-ecosystems can provide a basis for farmers to draw models of their farm enterprises and thus explore potential for the integrated use of different land and water resources. 'Bio-resource flow models', on the other hand, are seen as providing the engine for farm system transformation and the conceptual framework for quantitative ecological modelling. They observed that bio-resource flow modelling has the advantages of all RRA and PRA methods that use pictures to elicit, present and analyse information.

One set of participatory diagnostic techniques currently attracting more attention are those known as the GRAAP (*Groupe de Recherche et d'Appui pour l'Autopromotion Paysanne*) method (GRAAP, 1987). These techniques are seen as one way to expand the PRA repertoire and possibly to bring together what are regarded as distinctive Anglophone and Francophone traditions. They were designed to catalyse self-development through a process of increasing self awareness: in principle

103

they enable participants to understand the causes and consequences of their situation and to prioritize actions by which it can be improved. This is achieved through a dialogue based on a series of questions and the use of visual aids, and a continuing process of dialogue is envisaged. The World Neighbors' West Africa programme uses a similar approach (Gubbels, 1989), posing a series of questions which help farmers with their own analysis (How does what you do differ from what your father did? What are the principal agricultural problems? What solutions have you already tried?).

While participatory diagnosis is widely used as a first step in the planning process for most technology development programmes, it is also understood by many that a successful participatory research programme requires continuous diagnosis which depends on the establishment of a dialogue between researchers and farmers. Fujisaka (1991) has even argued for detailed, systematic, day-to-day communication and interaction between researchers and farmers in order to optimize skills and contribute to the evolution of complex agricultural systems. The issue, as discussed in previous chapters, is how to manage the interface. While PRA tools have moved beyond their 'Rapid Rural Appraisal' origins,[20] their promotion for needs assessment activities is linked with assumptions about rapid implementation and analysis as compared with more conventional investigatory tools, and in particular, questionnaire-based surveys. They are not, therefore, necessarily helpful when the need is to establish a continuous process of dialogue and exchange.

One of the most widespread concerns faced by programmes using PRA tools to initiate a research process is (what has been to date) a poor link between the results of the diagnostic research and the subsequent research programmes. It has been suggested, for example, that participatory diagnosis in Bihar, India, was followed by a rather conventional set of experiments (M. Collinson, personal communication). Freudenberger (1992) suggested that this reflects an evolution of tools to generate information on local knowledge which has been far faster than the collective willingness to change perspectives in response to that information. The problem of data management has already been mentioned. On the other hand, some programmes have found PRA mapping and diagramming exercises particularly useful in linking diagnostic activities to subsequent research. In a recent exercise, for example, ICIPE used a mapping exercise to evaluate community decision-making in relation to the placement of tsetse traps (Omolo et al., 1993).

One of the key criticisms of farming systems research was the

---

[20] Scoones and Thompson, 1992, for instance point out that the emphasis is no longer on rapid and cost effective but on 'relaxed' approaches that do not suffer from the danger of being rushed and wrong.

perceived lack of attention to differentiation within communities. The same critique is already being made of some farmer participatory research programmes. Thus, Ewell (1988) in his review of national research systems concluded that despite an increase in participation, the selection of farmers as collaborators is a chronically weak area. Most of the programmes he reviewed relied primarily on *ad hoc* procedures which were biased in favour of large and influential farmers. Cromwell and Wiggins (1993) reached essentially the same conclusion: there were only a few cases where agencies specifically targeted poor farmers. None of the agencies had investigated traditional community seed distribution mechanisms in any detail and few had attempted to trace how far project seed had spread and to which groups. The continuing relevance of this issue is highlighted by Sperling and Loevinsohn (1993) who observed that the poor are not favoured in indigenous seed networks: rather, they are considered to be undesirable partners.

At the same time, most diagnostic studies highlight differences within communities and wealth ranking is a well-established PRA tool (Grandin, 1988; Welbourn, 1991). Nevertheless, as a number of reports indicate, these issues are not always addressed during implementation. As Ashby (1992) points out:

Participatory methods are efficient means of reaching the poor and disadvantaged but equitable only if certain conditions to ensure their involvement are fulfilled.

Possibly the most common strategy used to ensure the participation of women for instance is to implement separate women's programmes. Thus, women are involved in a number of varietal selection programmes such as the previously cited work of CIAT, and similar programmes at ICRISAT in India. In fact, the whole problem of how to address social differentiation is not widely discussed. There appears to be some agreement that it is difficult to target programmes specifically to meet the needs of the poorest people or groups considered to be especially disadvantaged, without also providing for others, and reference is made to the usurpation of activities by unselected partners.[21] However, BRAC, the Grameen Bank and other NGOs in Asia have implemented development programmes in such a way as to potentially benefit the poorest, and several NGOs have implemented separate women's development programmes.

Those wishing to work with farmers as researchers are faced with other

---

[21] Olivier de Sardan (1990) notes that it is presumptuous of outsiders to think that the 'poor' are not linked with other groups or are simply waiting for outsiders to effect a change in their status.

problems. As discussed in Chapter 5, the choice of research partners is complex and must depend on the specific objectives. Some of the programmes presented in Chapter 4 did screen participants as to their resource base once a group of interested people had volunteered or had been selected by the community. On the other hand, the participants in the ATIP programme in Botswana were selected without any consideration of their resource base, but the project concluded that they were representative of their communities (Heinrich, 1993).

Mosse (1993) brings the discussion back to the more general issue of the inevitably limited participation of all segments of a community in PRA activities, and highlights what he argues are mistaken assumptions about community accessibility. He suggests that the appraisal is almost always based on interaction with a limited number of individuals who serve as brokers or mediators between the community and outsiders.[22] Selective presentation of opinion is likely to be exaggerated and minority and deviant views are often suppressed, especially in public. Thus, the perspectives of the most powerful community members are likely to dominate: they have the ability to identify personal interests with general ones, to ensure that they fall within the project.

With respect to the participation of women in PRA activities, Mosse refers to the now well-known problems of time, location and collective presence which are frequently incompatible with the structure of women's work roles, while cultural rules often limit their contact with strangers in public places. Although proponents of PRA have argued that it is not, unlike 'scientific methods', culture bound, Mosse argues that 'participatory rhetoric' can be conceived of as devious: notions of informality are culturally defined and situation-specific, and the paraphernalia of PRA – charts, maps, etc. – may mystify rather than entice participation. It is also suggested elsewhere that exercises in participatory diagramming and mapping have a natural appeal to outsiders with limited competence in the local language (which may be one significant reason why they have become so popular) (KRIBHCO, 1992). Finally, Mosse argues that public and collective events emphasize the general over the particular, while it is the specific which is essential for identifying issues of differentiation and difference. Many communities

---

[22] A study in Badeku, in Western Nigeria, by Peter Ay (reported in Hoffman, 1990) details how these intermediaries were selected and subsequently played a role in creating an 'illusion of communication between projects and their client groups'. As he points out, projects naturally turn to community members who already have experience with formal institutions – those who have attended school, worked in towns or other regions, taken part in cooperative organizations or have been leaders of religious groups. These people play a decisive role in creating illusions about the project. They, along with project workers, are under pressure from the rest of the community (and even neighbouring communities) to make the project succeed.

also do not habitually demonstrate poverty to outsiders. Clearly, these issues can be addressed over time if knowledge of the community increases. Within research programmes, which are usually short term, the problem is much more difficult to resolve.

In general, it may be said that the techniques associated with PRA have facilitated a closer relationship between researchers and farmers, yet there is growing documentation of problems associated with moving participatory planning beyond the development of a list of obvious needs (which is frequently the output of RRA and PRA exercises). Concerns are, therefore, being expressed about the way in which the techniques and tools have been popularized and about the underlying assumptions. These assumptions are now seen by a number of people as closely associated with significant implementation problems. Perhaps a more damaging criticism is that PRA, as it is now often implemented, is largely technique-led: there is a tendency to go out with a fixed set of techniques which become the framework of the activity. This is particularly ironic in the sense that PRA approach emerged, in part, in response to an over-emphasis on techniques and technology. Training and promotional materials give the mistaken impression that relevant planning information comes in the form of a set of completed (technique-led) PRA exercises.

Like all methods and tools, the effectiveness of PRA tools and methods depends on the level of competence with which they are handled. In the case of participatory activities, one key is communication skills, which are not seriously addressed in any of the PRA documentation. Thus, while the PRA literature places considerable emphasis on learning how to use particular tools for looking at time and space for example, far less attention is given to how to organize and facilitate meetings (which are integral to many of the PRA tools).

Finally, in contrast with the problem of lack of sufficient particularism necessary to address equity issues in some of PRA techniques raised by Mosse, there is the opposite problem of how to move from the individual village situation to the more general perspective of an area or the wider community. This is the location-specificity problem which all village level studies face. One solution being utilized by some programmes is to repeat the diagnostic exercise, using the same set of PRA tools, in a number of villages. The problem then becomes one of drawing this material together (the problem of data management referred to earlier). In this scenario, the diagnostic process is long and expensive, two characteristics of conventional approaches which are not usually associated with PRA techniques. Consequently, at least in one of these programmes reviewed for this study, different people completed the work in different villages, thus making comparisons between villages extremely difficult. By following a set routine, this procedure also goes against the flexible and iterative nature of the participative diagnostic process which is emphasized in the PRA literature.

The apparent dilemma is not therefore inherent to the tools themselves. It is, however, possibly related more to the dichotomy hypothesized between PRA (participatory 'empowering' techniques), viewed as part of the 'new professionalism' (Chambers, 1992) and questionnaires and individual interviews, viewed as non-participatory, extractive and disempowering. Faced with this evaluation, it appears that some practitioners are avoiding the more usual social science approach of moving from the detailed, iterative studies using open ended discussions and participant observation, to cross-checking using questionnaires, which might be the more appropriate strategy. Cross-checking is referred to as 'triangulation' in the PRA literature but refers specifically to the PRA exercise itself rather than to subsequent research possibly using different tools and approaches.

On-farm trials as a component of farmer participatory research

The participation of farmers in on-farm trials is certainly not new. There is, however, new emphasis on the level and mode of participation: a number of examples of enhanced participation in on-farm trials were reported at the IDS workshop in 1987 (Fernandez and Salvatierra, 1989; Colfer, 1989; Sumberg and Okali, 1988) and others continue to be reported (Defoer *et al.*, 1992). For example, the now ten year old Small Ruminant Collaborative Research Support Programme to improve Andean Sheep and Alpaca Production in Peru uses a participatory methodology to involve farmers in problem definition, trial design and implementation, as well as in recording and analysing results (McCorkle, 1990). More generally, farmers now have some choice in which innovations to test, are often consulted on trial design and are usually involved in trial evaluation.

Such is the current emphasis on farmer participation in trials that they are almost universally used as the litmus test of participation, both by the projects themselves and by evaluators and reviewers. Hence, whereas Farrington and Martin (1990) noted the lack of detailed information on 'process' coming from participatory research programmes, there are now detailed reports of the levels of participation in trials beginning with trial conception, and moving through monitoring, recording of results and final evaluation. The Farm Africa programme in Ethiopia divides trial operations into seven steps for this purpose and notes that these could be further subdivided. This development is a far cry from the simple farming systems 'researcher-designed or managed', 'farmer-designed or managed' trial categories with which many are familiar. And while there is a danger that the very flexibility and openness required for collegiate research of any kind will be lost by attempts to structure processes at this level, current trends reflect a greater appreciation of the need to consider farmer involvement in decision-making as a key test of participation. The dilemma, however, relates to the level of participation, the implications of greatly increased participation, and methods of enhancing farmers' experimental capacity without controlling and stifling it.

We have already presented what appear to be two contrasting ways in which farmer experimentation is being approached: one which tries to 'strengthen' farmers' capabilities by teaching more formal research and analysis skills and techniques to replace existing practice, the other which simply feeds or stimulates farmers' own research. Available documentation indicates that the former approach is both more common, and preferred by researchers and development-oriented organizations alike.

Baker (1991) aptly describes the situation from the researchers' point of view: since farmer experiments do not generally involve control plots and rarely involve formal measurement or multiple sites, they have limited value for extrapolation to other sites and do not provide the information necessary to convince others. For Tripp (1991) the difference between the two approaches is clear: one represents the application of rigorous agricultural science, while the other 'the haphazard offering of innovations and ideas'.

The issue which programmes face is one of reconciling participation with researcher control. While this was also a problem for on-farm research activities within farming systems programmes, it is reasonable to expect something which distinguishes trials undertaken by farmer participatory research programmes from those of previous farming systems research. The dilemma is greater in the case of farmer participatory research because of its wider objectives. However, it is clear from the previous discussion that not only have levels of participation increased, but the objectives of on-farm trials have, in many cases, changed from the conventional ones of testing technologies within the given local context. The stated aims of many projects are now twofold: to *complement* existing farmer experimentation, and to *enhance* farmers' ability to use and understand the experimental methods used by professional researchers. Thus, a basic distinction is being made between the transfer of specific practical information, technology or skills on the one hand, and increasing farmers' abilities to investigate new knowledge and information on the other.

Support for formal trials appears throughout the literature on farmer participatory research. Gubbels (1989) reporting on experience from Burkina Faso, Mali and Togo observed that the local research process is not systematic or organized. Farmers innovate individually and copy informally: there is no group discussion of problems. Lightfoot (1987) suggested that indigenous research is slow. These characteristics are regarded as problematic from a participatory perspective (presumably because they make the implementation of project activities more difficult). There is a slightly different view from India where Maurya (1992) has argued that the objective of NDUAT's now eight year old on-farm programme at Faizabad, has been to induce and strengthen *the informal research capability of farming communities*, which has been eroded over the years. However, van der Ploeg (1989) is not convinced that local knowledge can lend itself to standardization which is implicit in the strengthening activities.[23]

Thus, although farmers' own experimental skills are promoted as one of the underlying justifications for increased participation of farmers in the research process, in many cases these skills are considered inadequate and in need of improvement (strengthening or enhancement). It is even argued that 'greater participation will only come through building farmers skills in experimentation' (Lightfoot *et al.*, 1993). Training of farmers in the techniques of experimentation is now a common feature of participatory research programmes, and as noted already, several handbooks covering participatory experimentation are now available for trainers. Thus, even though documentation from World Neighbors in West Africa talks of farmers designing their own trials, in fact, farmers were guided through a dialogue which led to all villages arriving at a similar conclusions (Gubbels, 1989). Following earlier work in Central America reported by Bunch (1989), farmers were taught how to accurately stake out trial plots, etc., and a network of farmer experimenters (*'paysans essayeurs'*) who receive additional training, including literacy, specifically to improve the recording of trial results was set up. These resemble the 'self-experimenting village groups' discussed by de Jager (1991) in Northern Ghana.

Despite what appears to be the overwhelming support for standardized trials, they present numerous problems which are now all too familiar to on-farm researchers. Even with the benefits of standard designs and statistical rigor, conventional on-farm trials are plagued with variability. In addition to the usual problems of trial placement in marginal fields, poor maintenance and incompatible treatments, there are also varying levels of farmer and researcher interest in and ability to interpret the outcomes (Box, 1987; Sperling, 1992). In fact, some have gone so far as to suggest that more formal on-farm trials compare poorly with farmers' own trials, which generally permit a straightforward interpretation of

---

[23] Stolzenbach (1992a) even concluded that it is over-optimistic to think that farmer experimentation can be improved, and thus argues against a straightforward scientification of farmers' research: 'pragmatism and flexibility do not do well with systematization'

results[24] (in the sense that they are more realistic even if they are not always easy to 'read'), meaningful to both the farmer and researcher (Sperling, 1992; Sperling and Loevinsohn, 1993).

While there are those who hold the view that it is not possible to improve farmers' existing research capacity in this way, reports from some programmes suggest that they are attempting to bring together the benefits of both 'scientific' and farmers' own trials. For example, trials design and protocols used by COOPIBO in Rwanda have to be similar to farmers' informal research while at the same facilitating an assessment according to agreed criteria (Stassart and Mukandakasa, 1992). The trials should also guarantee a real dialogue between the 'expert farmers' and the 'expert technicians'. In their review of Farm Africa's work in Ethiopia, Biggs and Pound (1992) argued along similar lines. They recorded the fact that trials were modified (simplified) according to farmer requests after the first season; noted trade-offs between statistical rigour and farmer ownership (in a participatory sense); and observed that the needs of researchers should not be allowed to override those of the participating farmers. Nevertheless, they stressed that farmers' research should follow scientific principles – uniformity of conditions between treatments, non-confounding of treatments, replication and adequate plot size – all of which permit an analysis of stability of response over seasons and locations. They argued that these are all concepts that farmers can readily understand and incorporate into their on-going informal research. They also noted that recording procedures should be designed within the capabilities of farmers, but to a standard which would enable results to be analysed at a scientifically useful level. On the other hand, with technologies about which farmers have no knowledge, only researchers are expected to be involved in trial design.

Similarly, the ActionAid Research Unit in Uganda describes their trials as 'problem-solving experiments' and hence, 'in the areas of trial design and evaluation it is especially important to encourage farmers to apply basic scientific principles'. The programme began by leaving farmers to design trials as they wanted. However, since replication is regarded as critical for cross-checking, and gives researchers confidence in the results, farmers are advised, trained and assisted in the establishment of on-farm trials. Over time, therefore, it is expected that the trials will take on a more 'scientific look' (i.e., variability within and between trials will be

---

[24] This question of 'ease of reading' is discussed within the collaborative CIAT programmes in relation to the farmers' check. In their joint PNL/Mulungu (Zaire) programme, the researchers documented how farmers in South Kivu who were experimenting rarely felt it essential to compare two treatments side-by-side at the same time. 'The check proved rather to be a type of running summation in their heads: e.g.how the treatment (for example, a variety) performed over many seasons, in different fields, and under different management practices'(CIAT, 1992).

reduced). Farmers are also involved in recording and evaluating trial results.

Others provide similar guidelines to 'enhance the validity of results', while at the same time emphasizing the fact that final control should be left with the farmers. Thus van der Bliek and van Veldhuizen (1993) suggested that improvements to traditional experimentation may be suggested by outsiders to enhance the validity of results, while still leaving final control to the farmers. They also listed minimum requirements for improved farmer experimentation put together during a participatory technology development workshop involving researchers and extension personnel: experimentation should be limited to one variable at a time while all other variables should be controlled (some participants however suggested that it is sufficient to be aware that other variables may not be constant between test plot and control); the presence of a control plot (or control group of animals); five repetitions, either on one farm or spread over several farms; proper demarcation and measurement of test plot/animals; small experimental plot to decrease risks; proper measurement of yields of experimental plots; and monitoring of costs and income associated with both experimental and control plots.

The alternative possibility of not controlling the design of trials in any way has already been discussed. The FarmLink, SAVE and Chivi projects, and the integrated pest control research of the Panamerican Agricultural School, rely almost totally on farmers' own experimental skills. In these cases, questions of stability of response, replicability and statistical analysis are not posed. The assumption is that farmers are able to effectively evaluate alternatives and that there is little value in a parallel evaluation system which primarily serves the needs of the implementing agency. These programmes have done little if any training of farmers in experimental methods.

Few researchers have looked at trials in terms of specific information needs at different points in the technology development cycle. Certainly there is a sense in many of the reports that farmer participatory research and on-farm research more generally deals with what might be described as 'nearly finished' technologies. Thus McCorkle et al. (1988) gave the impression that if farmers have to adapt a technology, the research system is not working well. Janssen et al. (1991) appear to agree, since they suggest that if farmers innovate with suggested technologies, there must be inadequacies in the way research priorities are set. In contrast, Fujisaka (1993), also discussing farmer adaptation, argues that it demonstrates the flexible way in which farmers will adopt an interesting idea. When adaptation is observed it provides a view of the likely adopters.[25]

As indicated previously, many farmer participatory research projects work in marginal areas which have not been the target of sustained agricultural research, and focus on innovative agro-ecological approaches. Thus, in most cases there is little 'finished' technology available. The question then becomes, what kind of on-farm testing is called for (if any at all) when researchers are interested in working with farmers on 'notional' technologies? In many ways the early release to farmers of promising crop varietal material resembles the testing of notional technologies. As Maurya et al. (1988) noted, this is one way in which germplasm screening can take greater account of the diversity of actual farm conditions. The idea of a 'working model' discussed by Sumberg and Okali (1988) also seeks to include a range of diverse conditions and views early in the technology development process. Andrews et al. (1992) support an approach based on the provision of working models, arguing that it is not necessary to provide farmers with finished bio-control techniques, as 'it may be sufficient to provide them with key missing information' and let them apply the new information locally, essentially developing their own local technologies. Bentley (1992a) talks of giving farmers new, culturally appropriate concepts and then 'leaving them alone to do their own research'. Fujisaka et al. (1993a) describe the researchers' role in these instances: they initiate the transfer of a potentially valuable idea or element and then monitor farmers' progress in solving problems. For both Bentley and Andrews (1991) the key questions with this approach are: will sufficient numbers of farmers use this information and, can researchers effectively backstop farmers?

This approach would seem to fit with other current views. Röling (1986), for example, emphasizes the value to farmers of knowledge and information, and suggests that 'extension has to be about helping farmers to decide for themselves and strengthen their research and farming capabilities rather than about transferring technologies and recommendations'. Nonetheless, researchers (and many development organizations) have generally been unwilling to release technologies early enough for farmers to have an impact: they have too often seen their role in terms of prescribing fully developed systems or technology. The obvious result is that farmers are unable to determine early on whether or not a particular line of research has anything interesting to offer. The usual rationale is that unproven technologies and varieties are too risky for farmers. However, this flies in the face of the first principle of farmer

---

[25] In the specific case of hedgerow planting, those interested in adapting the technology had sufficient sloping land for soil loss to be a problem and few opportunities for off-farm income. Based on this experience a farmer decision tree model of the minimum criteria necessary for adoption of contour hedgerows has been developed (Fujisaka et al., 1993a).

participatory research: farmers are *constantly* experimenting with and testing unproven ideas and techniques (Johnson, 1972). Implicit in early farmer involvement in technology development is neither a format (e.g., standard trials) nor a scale (e.g., large enough to be risky).[26]

Alternatively, it has already been suggested by some that farmers might not be interested in early involvement, or would have little or nothing to contribute if the technology did not appear to lie within the bounds of their existing activities. However, most experience demonstrates that farmers are not at all averse to novel ideas and approaches. Researchers in the ATIP programme, for example, were surprised at the variety of technology farmers were interested to test (Heinrich, 1993). There are a number of writers who point to a more diversified approach to the development of new technology, an approach that does not assume that lack of control necessarily means a lack of useful information, and thus takes advantage of farmers' experimental curiosity. Thus Vigreux *et al.* (1991) describe the use of farmer 'innovation plots' to develop the basic idea of a 'shower nursery' that uses 'grey water' to produce vegetables and tree seedlings. Formal, replicated trials were also used to examine specific questions such as seeding density, the effect of management practices on seedling growth and production options for particular tree species of interest to the farmers. Neither approach necessitated large numbers of plots (the problem of more developed technology evaluation discussed by Menz and Knipscheer, 1981). These two approaches were eventually combined with the use of videos to engage a larger number of farmers (and extension personnel) in the experience.

Finally, while the review of current practice of farmer participatory research suggests that farmers have considerable involvement in formal research, not all experiences have been positive. Based on a perceived need for more precision in trial results, some projects have reduced the level of farmer participation. Bebbington and Thiele (1993) reported the case of CAAP in Ecuador which began trials on farms but researchers soon concluded that they could not control the research sufficiently. The organization subsequently bought land and developed an experiment station. Biggs (1989) observed a move by PIP, the national on-farm research programme in Ecuador, from a collaborative towards a contractual (i.e., less participative) mode of operation. This occurred, despite some viable and successful participatory activities, because scientists were increasingly working with farmers who were 'good collaborators': they had the ability to implement trials as required in order to minimize trial losses and ensure that reliable trial data were obtained. In other cases he reviewed, the movement away from participatory on-farm research reflected budgetary restrictions.

---

[26] Some exceptions are discussed by van der Bliek and van Veldhuizen (1993).

Technologies

[Farmer participation] appears to have the greatest likelihood of being continued...in crop management research, especially where technologies are knowledge intensive (e.g. integrated pest management or adaptation of wheat to new environments); in research on natural resource conservation and management, and germplasm improvement activities aimed at non-yield and other non-conventional characteristics (Fujisaka, 1992).

The question of whether farmer participatory research is more appropriate for looking at some types of technology than others has already been raised a number of times. The case of the development and testing of crop varieties is perhaps the most obvious example. New cultivars are considered a key means of increasing production amongst small farmers since they are comparatively simple to introduce and do not necessarily require large additional inputs. Both detailed research and casual observation highlight an intense interest among most farmers in new genetic material, and this may well be the most active area of farmers' own research. It is also in this area where significant advances in farmer participation appear to have been made (Maurya and Bottral, 1987; Maurya et al., 1988; Ashby et al., 1987; Sperling et al., 1993). Varietal selection is described by Stassard and Mukandakasa (1992) as one of the 'light' technical topics which are suitable for introducing the new participatory approach. Sperling et al. (1993) make a similar observation: there are few preconditions necessary for developing a client-driven breeding programme.

In contrast to germplasm improvement, the kinds of technologies associated with more general resource management, integrated pest management, agro-ecological and sustainable agriculture themes are often complex, difficult to investigate and seldom demonstrate results within a short time period. In this context a case has been made for greater control, long-term experiments and 'model farms'. However, some authors have suggested that it is just such complex technologies which require more farmer input because any particular, fine-tuned recommendation is unlikely to be widely adopted (Sumberg and Okali, 1988; Atta-Krah and Francis, 1987; Fujisaka, 1993). This would also seem to be the view of Lightfoot and Noble (1992), although they note that there is as yet no evidence that complex, farmer-developed aquaculture systems in which they are involved are necessarily sustainable.

There is also some indication that in a number of areas insufficient effort has been made to encourage client participation and therefore any evaluation of the value of the approach is difficult. This question is addressed directly by Van der Bliek and van Veldhuizen (1993) with respect to the development of tools, equipment and techniques. They concluded that:

there seems to be a lack ... of specific methods ensuring and stimulating participation of end-users and producers. Experimentation with the target group mostly took place through trial and error (p.23).

While they express the view that the kinds of technologies which they were considering (housing, weaving equipment, boats, animal traction tools and cooking stoves) might be difficult to develop through standard participatory techniques, they were of the opinion that the key factor determining 'success' was that all parties were open-minded and prepared to work together. They also concluded that different methods of integrating producers into this type of technology development were required. A number of writers have suggested that participatory research with livestock faces similar problems (see Okali and Knipscheer [1985] for example).

To date the base of experience is too narrow to conclude that the potential returns to farmer participation in research are directly related to the type of technology. We would not, therefore agree with Bentley (1990), who at one point identified niches for participatory research in dealing with the use of chemical inputs and the protection of 'wild lands'. In fact, there are some who argue that an important factor in the demise of farming systems research was its concentration on testing a small number of themes over many years, with only minor variations. Baker (1992) referred specifically to the long-term investments in fertilizer trials in high rainfall zones, and tied ridging and double ploughing in low rainfall zones. He suggests that the commitment of farming systems research to incremental change within the context of existing constraints was a 'slippery slope' leading to an inability to deal effectively with policy issues.[27]

Attempts to define specific problem areas or types of technologies which are more appropriate for farmer participatory research have been inconclusive, and will probably yield little of value. Clearly rural people have demonstrated a willingness to study and work with a wide variety of new ideas and practices, including totally new crops (not simply new varieties), associated processing techniques and new social arrangements associated with irrigation and storage.

---

[27] Although there were certainly a number of influential individuals who maintained that an important aspect of farming systems research was the development of whole new systems and the search for radical change (Simmonds, 1986).

Conclusion

This attempt to identify trends in the practice of farmer participatory research demonstrates a clear appreciation on the part of both research and development organizations of the need to move towards greater participation by clients in research. The shift towards working at the collegiate interface, however, is tempered by the balance sought by practitioners between two forces: increased client participation and less direct control or intervention by researchers. As we have already emphasized, farmer participatory research is about objectives and methods and the different emphasis given to each of these forces will be reflected in the character of the research task and the methods and tools used.

PRA methods and tools have been embraced enthusiastically as an alternative to questionnaire surveys which have been portrayed as providing little scope for holistic or qualitative responses. However, while these tools potentially provide for greater participation, they must be seen as only one part of a much wider range of methods, and probably require much more expertize in use than is commonly acknowledged. More attention to the management of mixed data sets of the sort produced by participatory rural appraisals is also clearly needed if the information is to be useful beyond the stages of description and diagnosis.

We have already identified an understanding of processes of informal local experimentation and information dissemination, and group processes in general, as critical for those interested in farmer participatory research. But PRA tools and techniques, and the increasingly standardized framework within which they are applied, are not making a significant contribution to the understanding of these processes. Thus, some farmer participatory research projects have concluded that there has been essentially no on-going farmer experimentation: no farmer experimenters or innovative farmers could be identified in the project area. Is this a reasonable conclusion? Can people live and farm in a variable environment without observing the effects of small variations in agricultural practice? We suggest that the answer to both questions is no, as the total absence of farmer experimentation would be the ultimate indicator of non-sustainability, as it would point to a fossilized, non-adaptive production system.

We suspect that part of the problem lies with the projects' conception and image of farmer experimentation and innovation. Rather than focus on individual 'experimental' actions or events which can be easily identified and discussed, the analysis of informal research should perhaps be more concerned with the mass of small experiments and *experience*, which over time supports the evolution of farming systems. The development of methods which will allow discussion and analysis of experimental activities at this level is the most critical challenge facing researchers who would like to profit from greater farmer participation.

Until these methodological issues are addressed, we conclude that the implementation of effective and efficient farmer participatory research will be severely hindered.

The proposition that farmers actively search for and evaluate ideas and options is, in many ways, the cornerstone of the argument in favour of farmer participatory research.[28] We have argued that this has significant implications for its niche in the research process as a whole: more involvement of clients earlier rather than later in the research process, and greater client control of the testing process. Our review indicates, however, that in general, most programmes are largely concerned with evaluating, adapting and extending technologies developed previously by the formal research system. With respect to more client control of the testing process, perceived problems associated with reduced researcher control are probably nowhere more evident than in the on-farm trial activities. While there are examples of less controlled experimentation, which is possibly the only approach to exploring the flexibility and limits of a notional technology, we must conclude that there is no clear, broad trend in this direction. One of the chief arguments for more control of trials relates to the need for 'scaling up' of technology. However, it can be argued that the debate over more or less standardization and statistical rigour of on-farm trials is of limited interest once a programme is taking place within a 'complex, diverse and risk-prone' environment (i.e., exactly where many farmer participatory research programmes are actually located). In such situations the 'recommendation domain' is, for all intents and purposes, reduced to the scale of a particular field or farm, and there is therefore no need for statistical techniques that, in principle, allow inferences to be drawn on a much larger scale.

From the evidence, we have also been unable to reach any clear conclusion about the appropriate technological niche for farmer participatory research for agro-ecological, composite or particularly complex technologies. The issues would appear to go beyond considerations of participation and levels of collegiality.

---

[28] Some may argue that it is empowerment of the poor.

7 Monitoring and Evaluation

Introduction

THIS WORK WAS initiated with an interest in developing monitoring and evaluation strategies, tools and indicators[29] that would be valuable for individuals and institutions that manage and fund farmer participatory research activities. It was hoped that the experience already gained by programmes on the ground could be used, and the particular interest was in those programmes which were working to create a 'collegiate interface' between formal research and farmers' own experimental activities (Figure 6.2). Two conclusions have emerged clearly from the review. Firstly that even though there is a move towards greater collegiality in participatory research activities, there appears to be less work at the collegiate end of the participation continuum, particularly working with the farmers' own research, than was anticipated. Secondly, few programmes have a monitoring and evaluation system in place which looks beyond the standard technical indicators of success. In fact, in the response to our request to practitioners for information about their experiences, most agreed that they were also struggling with monitoring and evaluation. This apparent weakness with farmer participatory research programmes is also cited by Clinch (1994) in his extensive bibliography of on-farm research.[30]

In this chapter, activities along the whole participatory continuum are looked at briefly to answer the question: what is being monitored and evaluated, and how? It is useful to structure the discussion of monitoring

---

[29] We use monitoring to mean the systematic collection of quantitative and qualitative information over time, and evaluation in the sense of the analysis of information (some from the monitoring activities) concerning the effects of project activities in relation to project goals and objectives. The discussion of the value of different types of project evaluation, including process and participant or beneficiary evaluation is well advanced and is not entered into here. A summary review of these can be found in Horton *et al.* (1993).

[30] All the manuals referred to earlier contain some reference to monitoring and evaluation. A few are specifically concerned with this issue, such as CIMMYT (1988) which looks at economic analyses, Muller and Scheer (1989) who specifically exclude economic analyses and Ashby (1990) who concentrates on farmer participatory evaluation.

and evaluation activities around trials, not only because these are a central feature of so many programmes, regardless of the level of client participation, but also because of the different ways in which they might be assessed. Chapter 8 then returns to the proposals for looking again at local experimentation and information networks for the design and evaluation of participatory research projects.

Monitoring and evaluation of technology

Our original view was that conventional indicators of the impact of agricultural research, such as increased crop yields, increased incomes and the spread of new varieties, would not generally be useful for evaluating farmer participatory research in marginal or low potential environments. In the first place, the magnitude of any expected changes would, in most situations, be very limited. In addition, the relatively short timeframes of most projects would reduce the likelihood of being able to observe and document evolutionary changes in practices or conditions. Finally, many programmes are addressing agro-ecological and sustainable agriculture themes, which are long-term by their very nature.

It is evident, however, that in some cases these and other 'traditional' indicators of change in agricultural systems are being used to assess farmer participatory research activities, and particularly in relation to crop trials. In most programmes information is collected during participatory diagnostic exercises and during the course of trials. The diagnostic information may be used to determine trial subject matter but, with the possible exception of the systems diagrams used by ICLARM and its partners, it is not clear that the diagnostic information is sufficiently focused to be useful in subsequent monitoring and evaluation.

With respect to the trials themselves, in some instances, the collection of quantitative information is considered so important that data collection methods and procedures are included in farmer training programmes. The main variables monitored are yield and input use, and results are evaluated in terms of productivity and income generated from the experimental and control plots.

Moving somewhat beyond this limited view, CIAT and ISAR in Rwanda will use information on costs of on-station and on-farm testing, impact at the farm level (number of varieties adopted and yield advantages) and contributions towards sustaining genetic diversity to compare a decentralized, farmer participatory variety development model with a classic, centralized selection model (CIAT, 1992).[31]

---

[31] The recent monitoring and evaluation literature does reflect an increased awareness of the wider implications of technology. As noted, however, few programmes move beyond an evaluation of the technical issues even though they may espouse wider aims. Posner

In general, however, little attention is given to the broader array of possible changes and effects (such as time saved, opportunities gained, decreased capital outlay or increased utility) which may be equally if not more important indicators of the impact of agricultural research, but which require the consideration of variables beyond the individual plot (Gilbert et al., 1993). In her recent historical study of several agrarian systems in Africa, for example, Berry (1993) argues that one of the most critical factors in determining the nature and extent of technical change is whether 'time is of the essence' which will conflict with African farmers' need for flexibility in managing their time.

Attention has been given to establishing criteria for monitoring and evaluating technologies associated with sustainable agriculture. In addition to production and profit data, the evaluation of some of these technologies requires environmental monitoring over a number of years and over large areas (Posner and Gilbert, 1991, but see also Hiemstra et al., 1992). This could include determining the relative dependence on purchased inputs, rates of run-off and erosion, loss rates of nutrients and water in the agricultural cycle and levels of genetic diversity. Change and impact must be assessed at the agro-ecosystem as well as the farm enterprise level, and some have argued that 'systems science tools' are therefore required (Lightfoot and Pullen, 1991). The ICLARM documentation on integrated aquaculture systems is significant in that it outlines a sequence of steps that include resource inventory and analysis, exposure to alternative techniques and monitoring of subsequent change in farming systems (Lightfoot et al., 1991). Since the objective is to change resource management strategies towards those that are less reliant on non-renewable resources, it is these changes which become the focus of monitoring and evaluation.

The review indicates that a large part of farmer participatory research is in practice concerned with the evaluation of and selection amongst technologies that are considered 'developed' or 'finished' (generally including planting material), and that in these situations the well-established evaluation criteria referred to above are highly relevant. Clearly, the character of the research and the research process, as well as the appropriate indicators for monitoring and evaluation, would be different if the focus was on the earlier (i.e., notional or preliminary)

---

and Gilbert (1991) link the more simplistic economic evaluations with Green Revolution-type or commodity programmes which took as their starting point, increased productivity of land and promoted a package of improved practices which included high-yielding varieties, fertilizer and improved management. Major indicators of performance were yield and maximum economic return per hectare, usually measured on-station. They argue that farming systems research evaluations cover not only production and maximum profit criteria but also additional economic indicators such as multi-enterprise optimization, risk analysis, calculation of transaction costs, returns to labour, and equity.

stages of technology development (Table 6.1). In addition, the question of monitoring and evaluating in a scenario where there is no formal trial plot, and where one is dealing with ideas, options or technologies that are more complex, has received far less attention.

Sumberg and Okali (1988), reporting on such a situation, asked: 'What outcome variables are of interest for evaluation of the technology when conventional on-farm trials are not involved?' Their interest was to gain an appreciation of the flexibility inherent in an alley farming model and thus to understand how, under what conditions, and for what ends the technology could be manipulated. They approached this initially (at the establishment phase) by assessing the conditions under which trees could be successfully established. Thus, emphasis was placed on maximizing the number of participants, with the explicit objective of increasing the range and variability in the circumstances in which the trees were planted.

It is more common for large numbers of participants to be sought for diffusion and verification studies than for work aimed at highlighting flexibility in implementation or further technical development. In the Rwanda example, three models of participation were compared: individual farmer experts, representatives of women's groups and community selection plots (CIAT, 1992). The community selection plots covering 50 or more farmers were rated high for 'community coverage' and possible country coverage, which are important scaling-up considerations, but relatively low for 'commitment to participation.' Similarly, ATIP's 'options testing groups' included 25 to 40 farmers compared with 'design groups' (which act to advise and assist researchers) of two or three members selected for their homogeneity (Norman et al. 1988).[32]

As is the case with quantitative indicators, it is important to determine how to arrive at a basis for comparison of qualitative judgements. In the alley farming case, the 'probability of successful establishment' was assessed simply by calibrating individual rankings of an evaluation team, using a few sample plots. This practice closely resembles matrix ranking which is fairly widely used in the evaluation of participatory testing activities, usually for comparing species or varieties. Stakeholder analysis (see Biggs, 1978) is carried out in a similar way but focuses on end users

---

[32] The particular focus of these evaluations, at least from the point of view of researchers, is also instructive. Their table of 'valid comparisons' refers to 'trials that were properly implemented and in which at least one plot produced some grain yield'. Other trials were examined separately and 'the reasons for failure are recorded and tabulated as important indicators of *field constraints*' (Heinrich, 1993).

rather than the technology.[33]

Most trials conclude with a final review, and these are usually based on data collected over the season and in discussion with the participant(s). In some programmes, these end-of-season reviews involve visits by farmers and researchers to a number of trial sites. Amongst the examples cited in Chapters 4 and 5, both COOPIBO (Stassart and Mukandakasa, 1992) and ATIP in Botswana (Heinrich, 1993) place considerable emphasis on these exchanges or cross-visits. In addition to giving opportunities to the visiting farmers, cross-visits are seen to provide valuable feedback for researchers that is used for planning the subsequent season's trials. It is not essential for information generated during cross-visits to be structured in a way that allows for strict comparison. Nevertheless, some relatively structured recording of information would seem to be invaluable for the planning of future activities.

Clearly, one aspect of monitoring and evaluation must be in relation to the effects of the change (i.e., innovation or technology) in question on the remainder of the system. However, the few identifiable attempts to evaluate the larger impact of farmer participatory research activities have focused on the level of technology adoption (and thus closely resemble the evaluation strategies of both commodity and farming systems research). ATIP in Botswana reviewed spontaneous individual adoption of a whole series of different technologies (Worman et al., 1989). Our review of the farmer participatory research literature indicates also that there have been few attempts to identify the range of interest groups associated with a technology and make a differential assessment of its potential impact on these different groups (using, for example, pay-off matrices as suggested by Biggs [1978; 1982]). On the other hand, there has been considerable discussion relating to the use of farmers' own criteria for evaluating technologies.

Monitoring and evaluation of social processes

Even though trials are in some cases promoted as part of a learning process relating to the building of local capacity and empowerment, most of the emphasis of monitoring and evaluation is on trial results and outputs, with relatively little on the groups (or individuals) themselves or the processes involved. In some cases, for example the ATIP programme in Botswana, improvement of the process is assessed by the percentage

---

[33] As illustrated by the work of ICLARM, some PRA tools such as maps and diagrams are being used for monitoring changes in systems. Rankings and matrices can also be used for all kinds of comparisons and evaluation. Some of the most enthusiastic support for the use PRA tools for monitoring and evaluation is provided by Chambers (1992) but Khan (1992) also concludes that the use of PRA for monitoring is a 'pioneer area', and that 'PRA is uniquely positioned to integrate quantitative and qualitative data.'

of 'successful' tests, a measure of the clients' expertize in implementing the trial protocol.

Monitoring of the processes associated with on-farm trials has been used to demonstrate a move toward more collaborative and collegiate relationships with farmers. Some have reported shifts from contractual to collaborative relationships based on changes in decision-making relating to trial design and implementation. In Zimbabwe, for example, Biggs (1989) noted that the design of trials was changed from blocks to strips because it made it easier for farmers and researchers to compare treatments. To some extent then, and similar to the experience with farming systems research, there is a tendency for the analysis of the relationship between farmers and researchers to be restricted to the interaction around the trials.

The ICIPE project in Kenya provides one example where group processes are the central focus of the monitoring and evaluation activities. In this instance, the technology is already developed, i.e., the traps are known to effectively attract and destroy tsetse flies. The research problem is to find ways in which 'communities' might organize themselves to develop and implement a control strategy using the traps. While a number of key technical and economic parameters such as livestock productivity, the level of tsetse challenge and incomes are being monitored, so also are the community organizations, largely through the documentation of specific events, meetings and decision-making processes.

Using the example of a less interventionist programme, and focusing more on our own particular interest in farmer participatory research at the collegiate interface, the FarmLink project in Egypt attempts to monitor specific processes that are associated with local innovation. The project's interest is the link between sources of information and farmers, and between farmers participating in link activities and other farmers. Monitoring focuses on the farmers' own assessment of the link,[34] the use of the information to inform subsequent decisions and the spread of link-related ideas in the community. The project literature contains no reference to evaluating the link activities from the viewpoint of the researchers and the impact that these may have, for example, on the research agenda.

While the principal focus of this review is programmes carried out within an agricultural research rather than within a broader development framework, we are nevertheless aware that empowerment as a larger

---

[34] The programme has developed a series of questions for monitoring the link process such as: How useful was the link? Did the farmer gain any information from the link? Is it possible (affordable, technically feasible etc.) for the farmer to adopt any of the ideas discussed? Will the farmer be able to repeat the link? Is the farmer going to try out any new ideas?

objective is closely associated with farmer participatory research, and indeed implicit in the collegiate research mode. For a large number of participatory research programmes, the focus is as much on political, social and institutional processes, as on the development and testing of agricultural technology. The discussion of monitoring and evaluation of social processes of this nature is clearly related to the growing body of literature on participatory or social development projects. This literature is concerned primarily with consciousness raising and political aspects of empowerment (Marsden and Oakley, 1991; Howes, 1992; Brown 1991; Khan, 1992; Moris and Copestake, 1993; Shetty, n.d.). Thus, some of the proposed indicators relating to group performance analysis, self management, problem solving and leadership (e.g. Shetty, n.d.). Although we have argued for a focus on a more narrowly defined set of objectives for farmer participatory research, this body of literature and experience has considerable relevance to the discussion.

Cromwell and Wiggins (1993) suggest that the continued emphasis on technology reflects the fact that some of the other aims of farmer participatory research, such as community empowerment and organization, are particularly difficult to assess. This is confirmed by looking at the social development literature referred to earlier. Brown (1991) goes further by pointing out that evaluations concerned with such processes as empowerment will be based on attitudes and normative premises which are necessarily highly subjective. He concludes that there are strong pressures on those involved in evaluation to give apparent theoretical validity to highly partisan attitudes:

> It is my contention that it is the normative bias within the social development movement that is at the heart of its present obscurity, and that as long as this orientation occupies a central place within the movement then the evaluation of non-material objectives will remain a field of enquiry resting more upon the faith of the true believer than on a coherent body of practical methodology (p.262).

Brown proposes that the expansion and consolidation of the local 'information system' rather than value shifts or changes in political relationships provides a more meaningful and less subjective indicator of social development. Van der Bliek and van Veldhuizen (1993) suggest that consolidated community networks are an output indicator of participatory technology development associated with the creation of favourable conditions for on-going experimentation and agricultural development.

Conclusion

The discussion of monitoring and evaluation procedures can only really take place within the context of specific types of research. We have already suggested some criteria to be used in a framework for these based on the continuum of participation (Figure 2.3) and the stage of technology design (Table 6.1). This is also a potential framework for project design. At the collegiate end of the continuum, following the actual practice of farmer participatory research as illustrated by this review, it is useful to include two alternative scenarios, one where the research involves farmers as colleagues in the researchers' own process and the other where the focus is on working with the farmers' own process.[35] Much of the existing work has focused on the less participatory end of the continuum, on situations where the technology is more developed and on testing of technology using fairly standard trial formats. The evaluation of activities at the collegiate interface, and working with the local innovative processes and information flows requires more information on these very processes including the nature of the links between farmers' own experimentation and local processes of information exchange – links without which the logic in favour of farmer participatory research falls away. Some programmes have begun to grapple with these issues and it has been suggested in discussions that a lot is known by programmes which have been in the field for many years. However, it would appear that little progress has been made in terms of the systematic collection and analysis of field information which can then be used for programme design and monitoring and evaluation.

---

[35] For the present we must assume that these are different processes and that there is no necessary connection between the two.

8 Future Directions: Linking evaluation indicators to project design

IT IS OBVIOUS that a meaningful plan for monitoring and evaluation can only exist in relation to clearly defined objectives and strategies. Examples given in earlier chapters indicate that the objectives of farmer participatory research are stated in terms of agricultural production or productivity, efficiency of formal research institutions, farmers' research skills, the interface between farmers' research and formal research and a number of objectives associated with the empowerment agenda. In all cases, farmers' own experimentation and information exchange processes must be central to high quality project analysis, design, implementation, monitoring and evaluation. The limited impact of farmer participatory research to date, and the general failure to effectively grapple with the monitoring and evaluation issue, reflect the lack of both a generally accepted conceptual framework and associated methods with which to identify, characterize and analyse farmers' own experimentation and information exchange.

It is in this light that we were forced to conclude that the original goal of this study – the development and testing of monitoring and evaluation strategies and tools *for more collegiate farmer participatory research* – was premature. Rather, the present need is for work that will lead to the development of a framework to be used for setting meaningful objectives, assessing alternative implementation strategies in the light of these objectives, and the identification of appropriate indicators for monitoring and evaluation.

Thus, the logic for a continued interest in the creation of a collegiate interface through farmer participatory research is as follows:

1. farmers' own experimentation and local information exchange have been and will likely continue to be central forces supporting the evolution of agricultural systems especially, but not exclusively, in marginal, diverse risk-prone areas;

2. interacting with, or creating a dynamic, collegial interface between farmers' own experimental processes and the formal research network may be particularly valuable to farmers in these situations;

3. the objectives and format of these interactions must take account of the nature and characteristics of (i) farmers' own experimental activities, (ii) local mechanisms and patterns of information transfer related to these activities, and (iii) the formal agricultural research system;

4. the characterization and description of farmers' own research and local information exchange will set the stage for the identification of both operational goals and evaluation indicators.

In the light of this logic, the simple model that follows identifies three major components that are central to the discussions of farmer participatory research: context, dynamism and outcomes (Figure 8.1). The proposition is that an understanding of (i) the nature and elements of dynamism (i.e., experimentation and innovation, information exchange, transfer, and transformation) in a particular situation, and (ii) the contextual factors which affect it, will enable both better programming decisions and point to those areas that will provide appropriate and practical evaluation indicators.

What is known about the 'dynamism' aspects of the model?

Farmer experimentation

Johnson (1972) refers to the 'propensity of traditional agriculturalists to undertake experimentation in the exploration of the unknown.' He accounts for the observable differences among farmers by citing: (i) adaptive response to ecological differences such as soil type, slope, etc., (ii) qualities and capabilities of the individual production unit (i.e., labour availability), and (iii) differences resulting from disagreement over the facts of the case or their meanings. The implication is that farmer experimentation plays a role in all three areas.

Critically Johnson makes a point of separating experimentation and risk: because of the small-scale at which farmers carry out experiments, they are seen to carry little real risk while preserving 'adaptive diversity.'

Rhoades and Bebbington (1991) identified three types of farmer experiments: curiosity experiments test an idea that happens to come to mind; problem-solving experiments seek solutions to old and new problems; and adaptation experiments test either an unknown component technology within a known environment, or a known technology within an unknown environment. Similarly, Stolzenbach (1992a) cites earlier work by Schön (1983) to identify three types of experiments. Exploratory experiments refer to actions undertaken just to see what will happen; hypothesis testing experiments are characterized by expectations about the

Contextual factors

Operating at different levels (local and national) and affecting innovative behaviour and the flow and movement of information:

• Degree of diversity, hazard and complexity of the agro-ecosystem;

• Strength of perception (and articulation) of opportunities, problems or constraints;

• Accessibility of new information, ideas, techniques, varieties, inputs etc.;

• Presence of social and cultural constraints;

• Strength of other forces motivating change (i.e., market opportunities; land pressure; land degradation etc.).

Dynamism

The farmer (as individual, family and/or community) to a degree determined partly by personality:

• Assesses available options and information;

• Observes, experiments, evaluates, discusses, adapts;

• Integrates new knowledge and innovation into on-going activities;

• Demonstrates, discusses, shares (or steals!) the experience, knowledge or innovation.

Outcomes

Which, over some unknown time period, will likely result in changes in:

• Production, storage and/or marketing practices;

• Allocation of available resources;

• Activity mix; Level or type of output;

• Productivity.

Figure 8.1. *A working model for situating farmers' own research and information exchange processes in their larger context.*

results of the action; and move-testing experiments are pursued to produce certain desired changes in the environment itself. Stolzenbach then indicates that practitioners such as farmers gain tacit-knowledge (i.e., adaptive rationality and co-ordination skills) by 'reflection-in-action.' Using the idea of reflection-in-action, experimentation is seen as a 'continuous innovative element of farmers' craftsmanship,' and 'it becomes difficult to talk of "experiment" as a special action, separated from daily activities.'

Thus, an understanding of farmer experimentation should not be centred solely on activities which are readily identifiable or around those relatively rare individuals who are recognized within their communities as 'experimenters' or 'innovators'. Rather, it extends to that experimentation which is seen to be a much more common element of the farming experience (Richards, 1986; Johnson, 1972; Stolzenbach, 1992a). It is important to note that such a broad view of farmer experimentation is not necessarily in conflict with the observation made earlier that it is unlikely that an orientation toward and skills compatible with the notion of a 'research-minded farmer' would be evenly distributed within communities or populations. At the same time, farmer experimentation is not likely to be a 'community' process in the sense projected by much of the participatory research literature.

In order to consider an event or situation as farmer experimentation, certain conditions must be met, including (i) the creation, or initial observation of, conditions or treatments, and (ii) the observation or monitoring of the subsequent results or effects. In the light of this definition we can distinguish between two types of farmer experimentation. The first, which we will term 'pro-active', refers to the more or less systematic activities of individuals known within their communities as innovators or experimenters. Specifically, proactive experimentation implies that some conscious move is made on the part of the farmer to create specific conditions or treatments, and that subsequent observations are more or less systematic.

The second type of farmer experimentation, 're-active', has no systematically set-out objectives, treatments or observation criteria. Much of the 'experimental process' is probably left to circumstance or hazard which determines the context and particular conditions in which observation can create new understanding. Thus, reactive experimentation might also be termed 'proto-experimentation': it is at the margin of farming practice, where the ideal or norm confronts the vagaries of specific seasons and circumstances, and probably provides much of the basis for the long-term evolution of farming systems.

Farmer participatory research projects are rightly concerned with both types of farmer experimentation. Indeed it may be that the link between these two types of activity is of prime concern.

There have certainly been some attempts to observe and characterize farmers' own experimentation. Mills and Gilbert (1990), for example, conducted an 'innovation survey' in The Gambia using interviews which charted the origins and history of specific technical changes within the farming system. Reference has already been made to the work of CIAT and its partners in Africa. Stolzenbach (1992a) used both direct interview and a life history approach to identify the origins of change in farming practice. Richards' work in Sierra Leone relied on the classic, participant observation to document experimentation and innovative behaviour among rice farmers. In Zaire the PNL/Mulungu collaborative programme with CIAT has made extensive studies of informal experimentation with introduced technology, including factors such as which farmers, frequency and criteria for assessment (CIAT 1992). A key element recorded was the farmers' concept of 'check' which diverged from researchers'. 'Relatively few felt it essential to compare two treatments side-by-side and at the same time. The "check" proved rather to be a type of running summation in their heads...' (CIAT, 1992). They also calculated the percentage of farmers carrying out 'conscious experiments on select factors' which they deemed important. Do these kinds of experiences deny the validity of these statements? Is experimentation with specific material technology (such as seeds or new tools) always likely to be more conscious than experimentation with techniques? (These kinds of distinctions come close to the distinction raised earlier between notional and developed technologies). And is there possibly a difference between investigations into techniques affecting strategic as distinct from operational decisions?

We suggest that while these and other attempts have yielded interesting and valuable insights, there is a need for greater conceptual and methodological clarity if we are to assess the existence and characteristics of farmers' own research in a way that will be useful for programming and implementation decisions and monitoring and evaluation procedures.

An approach to this challenge is to focus on the contrast between norms and behaviour of *individuals* (since what is normal is directly related to the individual concerned). Thus, we can envisage a situational analysis which allows one to distinguish between what is normal practice (i.e., within the bounds of normal variation for a given farming system) and what is actually being done at a given time and place. This approach can be illustrated by three questions which also relate to Figure 8.2:

i.   *When does one plant beans?*
      (= boundary 1, or archetype or system norm)

ii.   *When do you normally plant beans in this field?*
      (= boundary 2, or 'normal' practice of the individual)

iii. *When did you plant beans in this field this year?*
   (= boundary 3, or 'actual' practice of the individual)

The differences between answers to questions 1 and 2 can be explained, following Johnson (1972), by adaptive response to ecological differences, qualities and capabilities of the individual production unit and disagreement over the facts and meanings. In other words, normal practice reflects, in part, the accumulated results and understanding from previous experimentation.

On the other hand, our hypothesis is that the difference between the answers to questions 2 and 3, between norm (in an 'average' year) and behaviour (in a specific year), reflects, *to some degree*, behaviour which does not meet the two criteria set out above in the definition, and one or both types of farmer experimentation. The element of 'hazard' identified by Richards (1986) is probably one of the most important factors motivating experimentation. It is expected that the outstanding variation over and above that accounted for by farmer experimentation reflects, in large part, reaction to hazard that does not meet the criteria for experimentation.

We do not expect farmer experimentation to look the same under all circumstances. Once the situational analysis yields some indication of the current type and intensity of farmers' experimental activity, the question will be to take account of how they relate to other technical, psychological, social, political or economic processes. These contextual factors will determine differences in type and intensity of innovative behaviour between individuals, communities and regions and each of

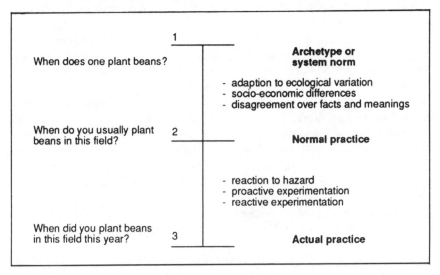

Figure 8.2 *A framework for the examination of farmers' own experimentation*

these levels must be considered. It is clear that there will be some scope for the use of a political economy framework in analysing the role of these factors vis-à-vis farmers' own experimentation.

The dialogue and reflection that these three questions will help to structure should let farmers and researchers, working together, come to a better understanding of the motivating factors, extent, and meaning of the farmer's experimental activities. This kind of analysis should create a solid base for decisions about programme and project strategy and activities, and set the stage for the identification of appropriate strategies and indicators for monitoring and evaluation.

Information exchange

The volume has focused less on information networks than on experimentation *per se,* although the operational emphasis placed by many programmes on encouraging farmer-to-farmer diffusion of information has been noted. Access to new information (ideas, techniques, varieties, etc.) was included in the model (Figure 8.1) as one of the contextual factors likely to influence the level of dynamism. At another level, the movement of new information is important for enhancing the significance of individual innovations, but also for strengthening both informal and formal research processes (see Röling [1988] writing on the importance of an active constituency for dynamizing the formal research process).

Much of the literature about farmer-to-farmer information exchange is really concerned with access to outputs of the formal research and extension systems. The poor record of extension in much of the Third World is attributed directly to its failure to institute a satisfactory process by which diffusion could occur. Yet, the spread of cocoa and cassava in West Africa provides incontestable evidence that rapid diffusion of technology can occur outside any formal extension system, and there are numerous other examples (e.g., Clay, 1974; Macdonald and Bartlett, 1985; Prain and Samaniego, 1986; McCorkle *et al.,* 1988).

While 'farmer-to-farmer', 'horizontal' and 'sideways' extension have received some attention over the last decade, there is fairly widespread, but often implicit, agreement in the farmer participatory research literature that autonomous dissemination processes are inadequate. Gubbels (1989) observed that farmers in Burkina Faso innovate individually and if an innovation is interesting, their neighbours may adapt it. However, there is no forum for discussing these ideas and developing a strategy at the level of community. Almy *et al.* (1991) based on their survey of the impact of formal extension services in the South West Province of Cameroon came to a similar conclusion and observed 'severe limitations to the distribution of material and information within villages'. Individual recipients often kept materials for themselves, and even the most 'open' farmers' groups excluded some part of their community. Many groups reserved new planting material for themselves even after they had multiplied enough for their own use, and 'in one village a few farmers had succeeded in keeping material away from everyone else for a decade' (p.81).

Pottier (1992), however, questions this view. He specifically challenges the proposition that farming techniques are 'family secrets' (i.e., the family locus restricts the onward movement of the results of experimentation because it limits the flow of genetic materials and management techniques [Dunkel, 1985]). Although Pottier agrees that pride and secrecy accrue to experiments, he emphasizes that they may be discussed with a few friends and will become public knowledge if successful. Likewise, McCorkle *et al.* (1988) note the existence of extensive information networks within rural Niger, and that the knowledge of individual experts is sought out by other farmers.

There is an implicit presumption in much of the related discussion that the movement of ideas and practices is a deliberate affair: thus, if the link between information and experimentation is essential, we might expect known 'innovators' to have particular networks that both feed and disseminate the results of their experimental activities. However, we suggested in the last section that farmers' own experimentation may be both pro-active (by recognized research-minded farmers and innovators) and re-active (by the population more generally in reaction to everyday events and circumstances). In relation to the reactive experimentation, it is possible that casual or *ad hoc* exchanges of information are significantly more important than for the known innovators.

Contextual factors are likely to affect the processes of diffusion as well as experimentation and we have already observed that these two are likely to be closely linked, the one feeding the other. Ashby's (1992) participation matrix referred to earlier (Figure 5.2) includes personality characteristics such as altruism, solidarity and leadership that indicate a willingness to pass on new ideas and information. Her model refers to the movement of information from an innovative individual, yet the rapid or widespread movement of the information could be blocked at any number of points beyond this first step (this would appear to be at the root of the concern expressed by Gubbels, if there is no forum for wider discussion and the differentiation within society extends to the movement of ideas).

It is difficult to define a clear procedure for the analysis of information flows and networks. As Long (1977) remarks, these phenomena are complex and their analysis requires an appreciation of how individuals operate in several, often geographically distinct localities. In addition close attention must be paid to how certain individuals and groups – gatekeepers or brokers – control important communication channels and access to centres of power and influence. The analysis of information flows relating to farmer experimental activities is particularly challenging as so little is actually known about the process of experimentation.

Network analysis provides one potentially useful framework, as it is concerned with finding explanations for behaviour based upon the patterned interconnections of network members. A key aspect of such studies is the definition of network boundaries. However, in Africa at least, where social networks are often fluid and contested, and members' positions within them vary according to individual patterns of participation in wider circuits of economic and social activity, the value and feasibility of boundary definition is highly questionable (Berry, 1993). In addition, our interest is not so much to explain behaviour, but to identify how people gain access to, or mobilize information, and to examine how this information impacts on the experimental process and ultimately a whole range of agriculturally related decisions.

One approach to the exploration of these issues would be to follow the lead of others in developing situational and network analyses to trace the local history of particular changes in agricultural practice. One might suspect that factors such as settlement pattern, levels of differentiation and commercialization will have a significant influence on patterns of access to and control of this information as well as the overall dynamics of its diffusion. It is also likely that new insights in relation to local information exchange will emerge from the study of farmer experimentation itself. It is not a question of understanding the experimental process in isolation, but of the links which feed ideas to and from it.

Conclusion

We have argued that the current interest in farmer participatory research has developed at the confluence of several major development themes: farming systems research, participation, empowerment, the importance of local knowledge systems, the role of NGOs, etc. Farmer participatory research has rightly generated considerable excitement, as it has attempted to move beyond the formal interactions that characterized much farmer participation in the early years of farming systems research.

Perhaps the most important difference between farming systems research and farmer participatory research is the latter's focus on the value and development potential of farmers' own research processes. Our review indicates, however, that few projects have yet developed a satisfactory approach to the interaction of formal and informal research activities. More often than not, projects have concluded that farmers' own research must be strengthened, enhanced or formalized before an equal partnership can develop. We have suggested that this situation can be attributed to a lack of clarity regarding the very nature of farmers' own research.

If farmer participatory research is to make a significant contribution to the establishment of a dynamic, collegiate interface between formal and informal research, new conceptual frameworks and methods that permit the description and analysis of local experimentation and information exchange will be required. Some groundwork has already been laid, and we have suggested how this might be expanded. It is only as these new frameworks and methods become available that the design, monitoring and evaluation of truly collegiate farmer participatory research programmes will be possible.

References

Abedin, Z, and Haque, F, 1987, 'Learning from farmer innovations and innovators workshops: experiences from Bangladesh', paper presented at the workshop on 'Farmers and Agricultural Research: Complementary Methods', Institute of Development Studies, University of Sussex, Brighton, UK, 27-31 July

ActionAid-Uganda/NRI, 1992, 'Farmer participatory research with Actionaid, Uganda: Initial project proposal', NRI, UK

ActionAid-Uganda//NRI, 1993, 'Quarterly Report, January to March 1993', Farmer Participatory Research Unit, ActionAid, Uganda

Adebo, S, 1992, 'Taro Root in North Omo Region', *FRP Technical Pamphlet* No. 2, Farmers' Research Project, Farm Africa, Ethiopia, June 1992

Agrawal, BD, *et al.*, 1978, 'Maize on-farm research project report', G,P, Pant University of Agriculture and Technology, Pantnager, India

Alemu, K, and Sandford, S, 1991, 'Enset in North Omo Region', *FRP Technical Pamphlet*, No 1, Farmers' Research Project, Farm Africa, Ethiopia

Almy, SW, Besong, M, Woldetatios, T, Poubom, C, Ateh, C and Mboussi, M, 1991, 'Farming systems research and the extension service: working across ministries in the South West Province of Cameroon' *Farming Systems Research-Extension*, Vol 2(3), pp 69–84

Altieri, MA, 1984, 'Diversification of agricultural landscapes – A vital element for pest control in sustainable agriculture' in Edens, TC, Fridgen, C and Battenfield, S, (eds) *Sustainable Agriculture and Integrated Farming Systems: a Conference Proceeding*, Michigan State University Press, East Lansing, pp 166–184

Altieri, M, 1987, *Agroecology, the Scientific Basis of Alternative Agriculture*, Westview Press, Boulder, Colorado

Altieri, MA, and Anderson, MK, 1986, 'An Ecological Basis for the Development of Alternative Agricultural Systems for Small Farmers in the Third World', *American Journal of Alternative Agriculture*, Vol 1(1), pp 30–39

Amanor, K, 1990, 'Analytical Abstracts on Farmer Participatory Research', Agricultural Administration (Research and Extension) Network *Occasional Paper* 10, Overseas Development Institute, London

Anderson, JR, and Hardaker, JB, 1979, 'Economic Analysis in the Design of New Technologies for Small Farmers' in Valdes, A, Scobie, GM, and Dillon, JL, (eds), *Economics and the Design of Small Farm Technology*, Iowa University Press, Ames, pp 11–29

Andrews, KL, and Bentley, JW, 1990, 'IPM and resource-poor Central American farmers', *Global Pesticide Monitor*, Vol 1(1), pp 7–9

Andrews, KL, Bentley, JW, and Cave, RD, 1992, 'Enhancing Biological Control's Contributions to Integrated Pest Management through Appropriate Levels of Farmer Participation' *Florida Entomologist*, Vol 75(4), pp 429–439

Anthony, KRM, Johnson, BF, Jones, WO, and Uchendu, VC, 1979, *Agricultural Change in Tropical Africa*, Cornell University Press, Ithaca

Arce, A, and Long, N, 1992, 'The dynamics of knowledge: interfaces between bureaucrats and peasants' in Long, N, and Long, A, (eds), 1992, *Battlefields of Knowledge: the Interlocking of Theory and Practice in Social Research and Development*, pp 211–246

Ashby, JA, 1987, 'The effects of different types of farmer participation on the management of on-farm trials', *Agricultural Administration and Extension* 25, pp 235–252

Ashby, JA, 1990, *Evaluating Technology with Farmers: a Handbook*, CIAT and the Kellog Foundation, Cali, Colombia

Ashby, JA, 1991, 'Adopters and Adapters: the Participation of Farmers in On-farm Research' in Tripp, R, (ed), *Planned Changes in Farming Systems: Progress in On-farm Research*, John Wiley & Sons, New York, pp 273–286

Ashby, JA, 1992, 'Identifying beneficiaries and participants in client-driven on-farm research', prepared for 12th Annual Farming Systems Symposium, Association for Farming Systems Research/Extension, 13–18 September, Michigan State University, USA

Ashby, JA, Quiros, CA, and Rivers, YM, 1987, 'Farmer participation in on-farm variety trials', paper prepared for the workshop on 'Farmers and Agricultural Research: Complementary Methods', Institute of Development Studies, University of Sussex, Brighton, UK, 27–31 July

Ashby, JA, Quiros, CA, and Rivers, YM, 1989, 'Experience with group techniques in Colombia' in Chambers, R, Pacey, A and Thrupp, LA, 1989, *Farmer First: farmer innovation and agricultural research*, Intermediate Technology Publications, London, pp 127–132

Atta-Krah, AN, and Francis, PA, 1987, 'The role of on-farm trials in the evaluation of composite technologies: alley farming in Southern Nigeria', *Agricultural Systems*, Vol 23, pp 133–52

Baker, D, 1991, 'Reorientation, not Reversal: African Farmer-based Experimentation', *Journal of Farming Systems Research-Extension*, Vol 2(1), pp 125–147

Baker, D, 1992, 'Inability of farming systems research to deal with agricultural policy', paper presented at 12th Annual Farming Systems Symposium, Association for Farming Systems Research/Extension, 13–18 September, Michigan State University, USA

Balakrishnan, R, and Nyirahabimana, P, 1992, 'Rwanda women's role in integrated aquaculture systems for resource sustainability', paper presented at 12th Annual Farming Systems Symposium, Association for Farming Systems Research/Extension, 13–18 September, Michigan State University, USA, pp 420–434

Bebbington, AJ, 1990, 'Indigenous agriculture in the Central Ecuadorian Andes: the cultural ecology and institutional conditions of its construction and its change', PhD thesis submitted to Clark University

Bebbington, A, and Farrington, J, 1992, 'The scope for NGO-government interactions in agricultural technology development: an international overview', *Agricultural Research Extension Network Paper* no 33, Overseas Development Institute, London

Bebbington, A, and Farrington, J, 1993, 'Government, NGOs and agricultural development: perspectives for changing inter-organisational relationships', *Journal of Development Studies,* Vol 29(2)

Bebbington, A, and Thiele, G, with Davies, P, Prager, M, and Riveros, H, 1993, *Non-governmental Organisations and the State in Latin America: Rethinking Roles in Sustainable Agricultural Development,* Routledge, London

Bell, KA, and Garrod, G, 1986, 'Farming Systems Approaches at Lumle Agricultural Centre, Nepal', paper presented at the 1st Farming Systems Working Group meeting, August 11–13, Pokhara, Nepal

Bell, M, 1979 'The exploitation of indigenous knowledge or the indigenous exploitation of knowledge: Whose use of what for what?', in 'Rural Development: Whose Knowledge Counts?', *IDS Bulletin,* Vol 10(2), pp 44–50

Bentley, JW, 1989, 'What farmers don't know can't help them: the strength and weaknesses of indigenous technical knowledge in Honduras', *Agriculture and Human Values,* Summer, pp 25–31

Bentley, JW, 1990, 'Facts, Fantasies and Failures in Farmer Participation', Symposium on Farmer Participation in Agricultural Research and Extension, National University of Honduras, October 16–20, 1989

Bentley, JW, 1991, 'The epistemology of plant protection: Honduran campesino knowledge of pests and natural enemies', in Gibson, RW, and Sweetmore, A, (eds) *Proceedings of a seminar on Crop Protection for Resource-Poor farmers,* Isle of Thorns Conference Centre, East Sussex, 4–8 November

Bentley, JW, 1992a, 'Alternatives to pesticides in Central America:

applied studies of local knowledge', *Culture and Agriculture*, Vol 44, pp 10–13

Bentley, JW, 1992b, 'An Alcohol Trap for Capturing Vespids and other Hymenoptera' *Entomological News*, Vol, 103(3) May and June, pp 86–88

Bentley, JW, 1993, 'What farmers don't know', *CERES* 141, May-June, pp 42–45

Bentley, JW, and Andrews, KL, 1991, 'Pests, peasants, and publications: anthropological and entomological views of an integrated pest management program for small-scale Honduran farmers', *Human Organisation*, 50(2), pp 113–123

Berlin, B, 1973, 'Folk systematics in relation to biological classification and nomencalture. *Annual Review of Ecology and Systematics*, 4, pp 259–271

Berry, Sara S, 1975, *Cocoa, Custom and Socio-economic Change in Rural Western Nigeria*, Clarendon Press, Oxford

Berry, Sara S, 1984, 'The food crisis and agrarian change in Africa: a review essay', *African Studies Review* 27(2), pp 59–112

Berry, Sara S, 1985, *Fathers work for their sons: accumulation, mobility and class formation in an extended Yoruba community*, University of California Press, Berkeley and Los Angeles

Berry, Sara S, 1993, *No Condition is Permanent: the Social Dynamics of Agrarian Change in Sub-Saharan Africa*. The University of Wisconsin Press, Wisconsin

Biggs, SD, 1978, 'Planning rural technologies in the context of social structures and reward systems', *Journal of Agricultural Economics*, Vol 29(3), pp 257–274

Biggs, SD, 1980, 'Informal R & D: the failure of farmers to adopt new technological packages entirely may be a sign of creativity rather than backwardness', *CERES* 13, pp 23–26

Biggs, SD, 1982, 'Institutions and decision-making in agricultural research', in Stewart, F, and James, J, (eds), *The economics of new technology in developing countries*, Francis Pinter, London, pp 209–224

Biggs, SD, 1983, 'Monitoring and control in agricultural research systems: maize in Northern India', *Research Policy*, Vol 12(1), pp 37–59

Biggs, SD, 1984, 'Awkward but common themes in agricultural policy', in Clay, EJ, and Schaffer, BB, (eds) *Room for Manoeuvre: an Exploration of Public Policy in Agriculture and Rural Development*, Heinemann, London, pp 59–73

Biggs, SD, 1989, 'Resource-poor farmer participation in research: a synthesis of experiences from nine agricultural research systems', *OFCOR Comparative Study Paper* No 3, ISNAR

Biggs, SD, and Clay, EJ, 1981, 'Sources of Innovation in Agricultural Technology', *World Development*, Vol 9, pp 321–326

Biggs, SD, and Farrington, J, 1990, 'Farm systems research and the rural poor: the historical, institutional, economic and political context', paper prepared for the 10th Annual Association for Farming Systems Research-Extension Symposium, Michigan State University, October 14–17

Biggs, SD, and Farrington, J, 1991a, *Agricultural research and the rural poor: a review of social science analysis,* IDRC, Ottowa

Biggs, SD, and Farrington, J, 1991b, 'Assessing the Effects of Farming Systems Research: Time for the Reintroduction of a Political and Institutional Perspective', *Journal of the Asian Farming Systems Association*, Vol 1, pp 113–131

Biggs, SD, and Pound, B, 1992, 'Farmers' Participatory Research: a Review of Farm Africa's Project in Ethiopia', ODG, University of East Anglia and NRI

Bingen, RJ, and Poats, SV, 1990, 'Staff Management Issues in On-Farm Client-Oriented Research', *OFCOR Comparative Study* No 5, ISNAR

van der Bliek, J, and van Veldhuizen, L, 1993, 'Developing Tools Together: Report of a Study on the Role of Participation in the Development of Tools, Equipment and Techniques in Appropriate Technology Programmes', GATE/ETC, Eschborn/Leusden

Boserup, E, 1965, *The Conditions of Agricultural Growth: the Economics of Agrarian Change under Population Pressure,* Allen and Unwin, London

Boserup, E, 1970, *Women's Role in Economic Development,* St Martin's Press, New York

Box, L, 1987, 'Experimenting cultivators: a methodology for adaptive agricultural research', *ODI Discussion Paper* 23, Overseas Development Institute (ODI), London

Brammer, H, 1980, 'Some innovations don't wait for expertise: a report on applied research by Bangladeshi peasants', *CERES*, 13(2), pp 24–29

Brokensha, D, Warren, DM, and Werner, O, (eds), 1980, *Indigenous Knowledge Systems and Development*, University Press of America, New York, USA

Brown, D, 1991, 'Methodological considerations in the evaluation of social development programmes – an alternative approach', *Community Development Journal,* Vol 26(4)

Brown, LR, and Wolf, EC, 1985, 'Reversing Africa's decline', *Worldwatch Paper* 65, Worldwatch Institute, Washington, DC

Bunch, R, 1982, *Two Ears of Corn: a Guide to People-centred Agricultural Improvement,* World Neighbors, Oklahoma

Bunch, R, 1989, 'Encouraging farmers' experiments' in Chambers, R,

Pacey, A and Thrupp, LA, 1989, *Farmer First: farmer innovation and agricultural research*, Intermediate Technology Publications, London, pp 55–67

Caldas, TSP, 1992, 'Indigenous and rural peoples knowledge and agricultural research and extension in Brazilian Amazonia', paper prepared for IIED/IDS Beyond Farmer First: Rural People's Knowledge Agricultural Research and Extension Practice Workshop, Institute of Development Studies, University of Sussex, 27–29 October

Carroll, T, 1992, *Intermediate NGOs: Characteristics of Strong Performers*, Kumarian Press, West Hartford

Chambers, R, (ed), 1979, 'Rural Development: Whose Knowledge Counts?', *IDS Bulletin*, Vol 10(2)

Chambers, R, 1989, 'Reversals, Institutions and Change', in Chambers, R, Pacey, A and Thrupp, LA, 1989, *Farmer First: farmer innovation and agricultural research*, Intermediate Technology Publications, London, pp 181–195

Chambers, R, 1992, 'Methods for Analysis by Farmers: the Professional Challenge', paper for the 12th Annual Farming Systems Symposium, Association for Farming Systems Research/Extension, 13–18 September, Michigan State University, USA, pp 420–434

Chambers, R, and Ghildyal, BP, 1985, 'Agricultural Research for Resource poor Farmers: the Farmer-first-and-last Model' *Agricultural Administration and Extension*, Vol 20, pp 1–30

Chambers, R, and Jiggins, J, 1986, 'Agricultural Research for Resource-poor Farmers: the Farmer-first-and-last Model', *IDS Discussion Paper*, No 220, IDS, University of Sussex

Chambers, R, Pacey, A and Thrupp, LA, 1989, *Farmer First: farmer innovation and agricultural research*, Intermediate Technology Publications, London

CIAT, 1991, 'Institutionalizing local leadership for farmer participation in agricultural technology generation and transfer in rural communities', Report of a special project, CIAT, Cali, Colombia, July

CIAT, 1992, 'Bean Research Project, Great Lakes Region', *Centro International de Agricultura Tropical (CIAT) Annual Report, 1992*, Rubona, Rwanda

CIMMYT, 1988, *From Agronomic Data to Farmer Recommendations: an Economics Training Manual*, CIMMYT, Mexico

Clay, E, 1974, 'Innovation, inequality and rural planning:the economics of tubewell irrigation in the Kosi Region, Bihar, India', unpublished D. Phil. thesis, University of Sussex

Clay, E, 1984, 'A more rational basis for policy: special planning units in Bangladesh and Sri Lanka', in Clay, EJ, and Schaffer, BB, (eds) *Room for Manoeuvre: an Exploration of Public Policy in Agriculture and Rural Development*, Heinemann, London, pp 33–48

Clay, EJ and Schaffer, BB, 1984, *Room for Manoeuvre: An Exploration of Public Policy Planning in Agricultural and Rural Development*, London, Heinemann Educational Books

Cliffe, 1973, 'Social sciences and agricultural development in Tanzania', In, Mbilingi, SM, *Agricultural Research for Rural Development*, Nairobi, East African Literature Bureau, pp 96–109

Clinch, N, 1994, *On Farm Research: an Annotated Bibliography*, NRI, Chatham, UK

Cloud K, 1987, 'Gender issues in AID's agricultural projects: How efficient are we?' United States Agency for International Development, Washington, DC

Colfer, CJP, with Agus, F, Gill, D, Sudjadi, M, Uehara, G and Wade, MK, 1989, 'Two complementary approaches to farmer involvement: an experience from Indonesia', in Chambers, R, Pacey, A and Thrupp, LA, 1989, *Farmer First: farmer innovation and agricultural research*, Intermediate Technology Publications, London pp 151–157

Conway, G,R, 1986, *Agroecosystem analysis for research and development*, Winrock International, Bangkok

Cornwall, A, Guijt, I, and Welbourn, A, 1992, 'Acknowledging process: challenges for agricultural research and extension methodology', paper prepared for IIED/IDS Beyond Farmer First: Rural People's Knowledge Agricultural Research and Extension Practice Workshop, Institute of Development Studies, University of Sussex, 27–29 October

Cromwell, E and Wiggins, S, with Wentzel, S, 1993, *Sowing beyond the state: NGOs and Seed Supply in Developing Countries*, ODI, London

Cruz, CRD, Lightfoot, C, and Sevilleja, RC, 1992, 'Rice-fish farming in the Philippines: the farmers' perspective', *World Aquaculture*, Vol 23(1), pp 52–55

Defoer, T, Erenstein, O, and Hussein, SS, 1992, 'From consultative to collaborative on-farm experimentation in the agrcultural development programme in Northern Pakistan', Paper received from the authors

Didier, P, 1993, 'La Recherche Système: Enquête d'elle même, *Recherche Développement: La Lettre du Reseau*, No 17

Dommen, AJ, 1975, 'The bamboo tubewell: a note on an example of indigenous technology', *Economic Development and Cultural Change*, Vol 23(3), pp 483–489

Dover, M and Talbot, LM, 1987, *To feed the earth: agroecology for sustainable development*, World Resources Institute, Washington, DC

Drinkwater, M, 1992, 'Central issues for farmer participation in adaptive research in Zambia', Paper adapted from document prepared for Adaptive Research Planning Team Workshop, Kasama, September 1991, Kabwe National Research Station

Ellerston, C, 1991, *The invisible woman*, United States Agency for International Development, Bureau of AFR/DP, Washington DC

ETC, 1992, *Learning for People Centred Technology Development: a Training Guide,* ETC, Leusden, The Hague, The Netherlands

Ewell, PT, 1988, 'Organization and management of field activities in on-farm research; a review of experience in nine countries', *OFCOR Comparative Study* No 2, The Hague, ISNAR

Ewell, PT, 1989, 'Linkages between on-farm research and extension in nine countries', *OFCOR Comparative Study* No 4, ISNAR, The Hague

Fairhead, J, 1992, 'Indigenous technical knowledge and natural resources management in sub-Saharan Africa; A critical review', Report submitted to NRI

Fairhead, J, 1993, 'Representing knowledge: the 'new farmer' in research fashions' in Pottier J (ed.), *Practising development: social science perspectives,* Routledge, London, pp 187–204

Farm Africa, Ethiopia, 1991, 'Annual Report: Farmers' Research Project', Farm Africa, Addis Ababa

Farm Africa, Ethiopia, 1992 'Report of diagnostic survey, Fagena Mata Peasants Association in Kindo Koysha Awraja', SOS Sahel, Farm Africa, MoA, Environmental Protection and Development (North Omo Region), January

Farm Africa, Ethiopia, 1993, 'Project memorandum: Ethiopia Farmers' Research Project – Stage 2', Proposal submitted to ODA

Farrington, J, and Bebbington, A, 1991, 'Institutionalisation of farming systems development: are there lessons from NGO-government links?', Paper for FAO Expert consultation on the Institutionalisation of farming systems development, Rome, 15–17 October

Farrington, J, and Bebbington, A, with Wellard, K, and Lewis, DJ, 1993, *Reluctant Partners? Non-Governmental Organisations, the State and Sustainable Agricultural Development,* Routledge, London

Farrington, J, and Lewis, DJ, with Satish, S, and Miclat-Teves, A, (eds) 1993, *Non-governmental organisations and the state in Asia: rethinking roles in sustainable agricultural development,* Overseas Development Institute

Farrington, J, and Martin, A, 1987, 'Farmer participatory research: a review of concepts and practices', Agricultural Administration Research and Extension *Network Discussion Paper* 19, London, Overseas Development Institute

Farrington, J, and Martin, A, 1990, 'Farmer participation in agricultural research: a review of concepts and practices', *Occasional Paper* 9, Overseas Development Institute

Fernandez, ME and Salvatierra, H, 1989, 'Participatory technology validation in highland communities in Peru', in Chambers, R, Pacey, A and Thrupp, LA, 1989, *Farmer First: Farmer Innovation and Agricultural Research,* Intermediate Technology Publications, London, pp 146–150

Finsterbusch, K. and van Wicklin, WA, 1989, 'Beneficiary participation in development projects: empirical tests of popular theory', *Economic Development and Cultural Change*, Vol 37(3), pp 573–593

Flora, CB, and Tomecek, M, (eds) 1986, 'Selected proceedings of Kansas State University's 1986 Systems Research Symposium', *Farming Systems Research Paper Series* 13, Kansas State University, Kansas

Freire, P, 1972, *Pedagogy of the Oppressed*, Penguin, Harmondsworth

Freudenberger, KS, 1992, 'Challenges in the collection and use of information on local livelihood strategies and natural resource management', paper prepared for IIED/IDS Beyond Farmer First: Rural People's Knowledge Agricultural Research and Extension Practice Workshop, Institute of Development Studies, University of Sussex, 27–29 October

Fujisaka, S, 1989, 'A method for farmer participatory research and technology transfer: upland soil conservation in the Philippines', *Experimental Agriculture*, Vol 25, pp 423–433

Fujisaka, S, 1991, 'Improving productivity of an upland rice and maize system: farmer cropping choices or researcher cropping pattern trapezoids? *Experimental Agriculture*, Vol 27, pp 253–261

Fujisaka, S, 1992, 'Somewhere beyond farmer first at the International Rice Research Institute', paper prepared for IIED/IDS Beyond Farmer First: Rural People's Knowledge Agricultural Research and Extension Practice Workshop, Institute of Development Studies, University of Sussex, 27–29 October

Fujisaka, S, 1993, 'A case of farmer adaptation and adoption of contour hedgerows for soil conservation', *Experimental Agriculture* (Forthcoming)

Fujisaka, S, Jayson, E, and Dapusala, A, 1993a, 'Trees, grasses, and weeds: natural vegetation strip choices in farmer-developed contour hedges', Submitted to *Agroforestry Systems*

Fujisaka, S, Dapusala, A, and Jayson, E, 1993b, '"Recommendation domain" again: farmer-to farmer transfer of a farmer-developed upland rice technology', paper submitted to *Indigenous Knowledge and Development Monitor*

Galema, A, and Mzigani 1992, 'Participatory Extension Experiences of Mifipro' in Stassart, P, (Comp.) *The view of field workers: 7 experiences of African agricultural Programmes supported by COOPIBO*, Papers written in preparation for the African exchange seminar on sustainable agriculture and farmers' participation held at Butare, Ruanda, 16 April–10 May, Phase 4

Gatter, P, 1993, 'Anthropology in farming systems research: a participant observer in Zambia, in Pottier J (ed.), *Practising development: social science perspectives*, Routledge, London, pp 153–186

George, J, Bebbington, A, Kpeglo, K, and Gordon, A, 1992, 'Sustainable agriculture and village extension project: a mid term evaluation', draft report submitted to CARE, Sierra Leone

Ghildyal, BP, 1987, 'Farmer evaluation of rice breeding material in rainfed lowlands of East India', IDS 1987

Gibbon, D, 1981, 'Rainfed farming systems in the Mediterranean Region', *Plant and Soil*, Vol 58, pp 59–80

Gilbert, E, 1990, 'Non-governmental organisations and agricultural research: the experience of The Gambia', *Agricultural Research and Extension Network Paper* 12, Overseas Development Institute, London

Gilbert, E, Norman, D, and Winch, F, 1980, 'Farming Systems Research: a Critical Appraisal', *Rural Development Paper,* No 6, Michigan State University, East Lansing

Gilbert, E, Phillips, LC, Roberts, W, Sarch, Marie-Therese, Smale, M, and Stroud, A, with Hunting, E, 1993, 'Maize research impact in Africa: the obscured revolution', Report prepared for the Division of Food, Agriculture, and Resources Analysis, US Agency for International Development

Goode, WJ, and Hatt, PK, 1952, *Methods in social research,* McGraw Hill, New York

GRAAP, 1987, *Pour une pedagogie de l'autopromotion,* [Groupe de Recherche et d'Appui pour l'Autopromotion Paysanne], Bobo Dioulasso, Burkina Faso.

Grandin, BE, 1988, *Wealth ranking in smallholder communities: a field manual,* Intermediate Technology Publications, London

Gubbels, PA, 1988. 'Peasant farmer agricultural self-development', *ILEIA Newsletter*, Vol 4(3), pp 11–14

Gubbels, PA, 1989, 'Un example d'autopromotion paysanne: l'experience de "voisins mondiaux" en Afrique accidentale', Special edition of ILEIA, January, pp 12–16

Gubbels, PA, 1991, 'An approach to promoting tree growing in Africa: the World neighbors experience in Northern Ghana, Towards self experimenting village groups' In Haverkort, B, van der Kamp, J, and Waters-Bayer, A, (eds) *Joining Farmers' Experiments: experiences in participatory technology development*, Intermediate Technology Publications, London, pp 49–54

Gubbels, PA, 1992a, 'Farmer-First Research: Populist Pipedream or Practical Paradigm? A Case Study of the Projet Agro-Foresterie (PAF) in Burkina Faso', paper prepared for IIED/IDS Beyond Farmer First: Rural People's Knowledge Agricultural Research and Extension Practice Workshop, Institute of Development Studies, University of Sussex, 27–29 October

Gubbels, PA, 1992b, 'Towards more Effective "Farmer-First" Research: Linking Theory to Practice in Agricultural Technology Development', paper prepared for IIED/IDS Beyond Farmer First: Rural People's

Knowledge Agricultural Research and Extension Practice Workshop, Institute of Development Studies, University of Sussex, 27–29 October

Handwerker, NP, 1973, 'Kinship, friendship and business failure among market sellers in Monrovia, Liberia, 1970', *Africa*, Vol XLIII (4), pp 208–301

Harwood, R, 1984, 'The integration efficiencies of cropping systems' in Edens, TC, Fridgen, C and Battenfield, S, eds, *Sustainable Agriculture and Integrated Farming Systems: a Conference Proceeding*, Michigan State University Press, East Lansing, pp 64–75

Haugerud, A, and Collinson, MP, 1990, 'Plants, genes and people: improving the relevance of plant breeding in Africa', *Experimental Agriculture*, Vol 26, pp 341–362

Haverkort, B, van der Kamp, J, and Waters-Bayer, A (eds) 1991, *Joining Farmers' Experiments: Experiences in Participatory Technology Development'*, Intermediate Technology Publications, London

Heinemann, E, and Biggs, SD, 1985, 'Farming systems research: an evoluationary approach to implementation', *Journal of Agricultural Economics*, Vol 36(1), pp 59–65

Heinrich, GM, 1993, 'Strengthening farmer participation through groups: experiences and lessons from Botswana', *OFCOR Discussion Paper* No, 3, The Hague, ISNAR

Heinrich, G, Worman, F, and Koketso, C, 1991, 'Integrating FPR with conventional on-farm research programs: one example from Botswana', *Journal for Farming Systems Research-Extension*, Vol 2(2), pp 1–16

Hiemstra, W, Reijntjes, C, and van der Werf, E, (eds) 1992, *Let Farmers Judge: Experiences in Assessing the Sustainability of Agriculture*, ILEIA Readings in Sustainable Agriculture, Intermediate Technology Publications, London

Hill, P, 1963, *The Migrant Cocoa Farmers of Southern Ghana: a Study of Rural Capitalism*, Cambridge University Press, Cambridge

Hill, P, 1970, *Studies in Rural Capitalism in West Africa*, Cambridge University Press, Cambridge, pp 21–29

Hoeper, Bernard, (ed) 1990, *Qualitative versus Quantitative Approaches in Applied Research in Rural Development*, proceedings of the Workshop at Sokoine University of Agriculture, Morogoro, Tanzania, 21–26 May, German Foundation for International Development, Bonn

Hoffman, V, (comp), 1990, 'Illusions of communication between projects and their target groups: a cautionary example in Nigeria', in *Rural Development Series: Agricultural Extension* Vol 2 *Examples and Background Material*, Deutsche Gesellschaft furechnische Zusammenarbeit (GTZ), Eichborn, pp 161–176.

Hope, A, and Timmel, S, 1991, *Training for Transformation: a Handbook for Community Workers*, Mambo Press, Zimbabwe

Horton, D, 1981, 'Potato: policy makers should consider the role this crop can play in a variety of ecological and socio-economic environments', *CERES*, January–February, pp 28–32

Horton, D, Ballantyne, P, Peterson, W, Uribe, B, Gapasin, D, and Sheridan, K, 1993, *Monitoring and Evaluating Agricultural Research: a Sourcebook*, Wallingford, CAB International with ISNAR

Howes, M, 1992, 'Linking paradigms and practice: key issues in the appraisal, monitoring and evaluation of British NGO projects', *Journal of International Development*, Vol 4(4), pp 375–396

Howes, M, and Chambers, R, 1979, 'Indigenous Technical Knowledge: Analysis, Implications and Issues', in *Rural Development: Whose Knowledge Counts?*, *IDS Bulletin*, Vol 10(2), pp 5–11

Hunter, G, and Bottrall, A, 1974, *Serving the Small Farm : Policy Choices in Indian Agricultural Development*, Croom Helm Ltd/ODI, London

ICIPE, 1992/3, 'Adaptive research to assess the sustainability of the ICIPE Tsetse Super Trap: an innovative tool for communuity-based management of tsetse and trypanosomiasis in Lambwe Valley', *Annual Report* for the period April 1992 to March 1993; Quarterly Report, April to June 1993

IDS, 1979, 'Rural development: Whose knowledge counts?', *IDS Bulletin*, 10(2)

ILEIA, 1989, *Operational Approaches for Participative Technology Development in Sustainable Agriculture*, Proceedings of a workshop ILEIA, Leusden

de Jager, A, 1991, 'Towards self experimenting village groups' in Haverkort, B, van der Kamp, J, and Waters-Bayer, A, (eds) *Joining Farmers' Experiments: Experiences in Participatory Technology Development*, Intermediate Technology Publications, London, pp 129–139

Janssen, W, Ruiz de Londono, N, Beltran, JA, and Woolley, J, 1991, 'On-farm research in support of varietal diffusion: bean production in Cajamarca, Peru, in Tripp, R, (ed), 1991, *Planned Changes in Farming Systems: Progress in On-farm Research*, John Wiley and Sons, New York, pp 215–230

Jiggins, J, 1984, 'Farming systems research: Do any of the FSR models offer a positive capacity for addressing women's agricultural needs?' CGIAR Impact Assessment Study, *Working Paper* 4, Washington

Jiggins, J, 1992, 'Don't waste energy in fear of the future', paper presented at the 12th Annual Farming Systems Symposium, Association for Farming Systems Research/Extension, 13–18 September, Michigan State University, USA

Johnson, AW, 1972, 'Individuality and experimentation in traditional agriculture', *Human Ecology*, Vol 1(2), pp 149–160

Kaimowitz, D, Snyder, M, and Engel, P, 1990, 'A conceptual framework for studying the links between agricultural research and technology transfer in developing countries', in Kaimowitz, D, (ed) *Making the Link: Agricultural Research and Technology Transfer Services in Developing Countries,* Westview Press, Boulder, Colorado

Kar, P, Arangzeb, SNH, and Mallick, RN, 1992, 'Farming systems research in Bangladesh: its progress and future strategies', 12th Annual Farming Systems Symposium, Association for Farming Systems Research/Extension, 13–18 September, Michigan State University, USA, pp 420–434

Kelly, GA, 1955, *The Psychology of Personal Constructs,* Norton, New York

Kerven, C, 1992, *Customary Commerce: a Historical Reassessment of Pastoral Livestock Marketing in Africa,* ODI, London

van Keulen, H, and Breman, H, 1990, 'Agricultural development in the West African Sahelian region: a cure against land hunger?', *Agricultural Ecosystems and Environment* Vol 32, pp, 177–197

Khan, Shakeeb, A, 1992, *Participatory Rural Appraisal,* Internal ActionAid document

KKU 1987, *Proceedings of the 1985 International Conference on Rapid Rural Appraisal,* Khon Kaen University, Khon Kaen, Thailand

Kotschi, J, Waters-Bayer, A, Adelhelm, R, and Hoesle, U, 1989, *Ecofarming in Agricultural Development,* Weikersheim, Margraf: GTZ

KRIBHCO, 1992, 'Kribhco Project Preparation Mission Document' Swansea, UK

Kuhn, TS, 1962, *The Structure of Scientific Revolutions,* University of Chicago Press, Chicago and London

Lehmann, AD, 1990, *Democracy and Development in Latin America: Economics, Politics and Religion in the Postwar Period,* Polity Press, Cambridge

Lightfoot, C, 1987, 'Indigenous research and on-farm trials', workshop on 'Farmers and Agricultural Research: Complementary Methods', Institute of Development Studies, University of Sussex, Brighton, UK, 27–31 July

Lightfoot, C, Axinn, N, John, KC, Chambers, R, Singh, RK, Garrity, D, Singh, VP, Mishra, P and Salman, A, (comp), 1990b, *Training Resource Book for Participatory Experimental Design,* Narendra Deva University of Agriculture and Technology, International Rice Research Institute (IRRI) and International Center for Living Aquatic Resources Management (ICLARM)

Lightfoot, C, Gupta, MV, and Ahmed, M, 1992 'Low external input: sustainable agriculture for Bangladesh-an operational framework', *NAGA* (the ICLARM Quarterly), pp, 9–12

Lightfoot, C, Noble, R, and Morales, R, 1991, 'Training resource book on a participatory method for modelling bioresource flows', *ICLARM Educational Series*, No 14

Lightfoot, C, and Noble, R, 1992, 'Sustainability and on-farm experiments: ways to exploit participatory and systems concepts', paper presented at the 12th Annual Farming Systems Symposium, Association for Farming Systems Research/Extension, 13–18 September, Michigan State University

Lightfoot, C, Pingali, P, and Harrington, L, 1993, 'Beyond romance and rhetoric: sustainable agriculture and farming systems research', *NAGA* (the ICLARM Quarterly), January, Contribution No 912

Lightfoot, C, and Pullin, RSV, 1991, 'Why Asian FSRE needs qualitative methods for integrating agriculture with aquaculture', *Journal of Asian Farming Systems Association*, Vol 1, pp 201–215

Lightfoot, C, Singh, VP, Paris, T, Mishra, P, and Salman, A, (comp), 1990a, *Training Resource Book for Farming Systems Diagnosis*, International Rice Research Institute (IRRI) and International Center for Living Aquatic Resources Management (ICLARM)

Lipton, M, with Longhurst, R, 1989, *New Seeds and Poor People*, Unwin Hyman Ltd, London

Loevinsohn, ME, Mugarura, J and Nkusi, A, 1993, 'Cooperation and innovation by farmer groups in Rwandan valleys', paper submitted to *Agricultural Systems*

Long, N, 1992, 'Introduction' in Long, N, and Long, A (eds), *Battlefields of Knowledge: the Interlocking of Theory and Practice in Social Research and Development*, Routledge, London, pp 3–15

Long, N, and Long, A, (eds), 1992, *Battlefields of Knowledge: the Interlocking of Theory and Practice in Social Research and Development*, Routledge, London

Long, N, van der Ploeg, JD, 1989, 'Demythologizing planned intervention: an actor perspective', *Sociologie Ruralis* Vol 19(3/4), 226–249

Long, N, and Villareal, M, 1992, 'Exploring agricultural development interfaces: from knowledge transfer to the transformation of meaning', paper prepared for IIED/IDS Beyond Farmer First: Rural People's Knowledge Agricultural Research and Extension Practice Workshop, Institute of Development Studies, University of Sussex, 27–29 October

Macdonald, IS, and Bartlett, AP, 1985, *Progressive Farmer Research*, Ian Macdonald Associates LTD, London

Marsden, D, and Oakley, P, (eds), 1991, *Evaluating Social Development Projects*, Oxfam, Oxford

Mathema, SR, and Galt, DL, 1986, 'Report on the process of group survey and on-farm trial design activity', Naldung village, Panchayat, Kavre District, Nepal, SERED Report No 2, Dept of Agriculture, Socio-Economic Research and Extension Division, Khumaltar, Nepal

Maurya, DM, 1992, 'Farmer participatory on-farm research methodology: a sustainable model', 12th Annual Farming Systems Symposium, Association for Farming Systems Research/Extension, 13–18 September, Michigan State University, USA, pp, 87–110

Maurya, DM, and Bottrall, A, 1987, Innovative approaches of farmers for raising their farm productivity, workshop on 'Farmers and Agricultural Research: Complementary Methods', Institute of Development Studies, University of Sussex, Brighton, UK, 27–31 July

Maurya, DM, Bottrall, A, and Farrington, J, 1988, 'Improved livelihoods, genetic diversity and farmer participation: a strategy for rice breeding in rainfed areas of India', *Experimental Agriculture*, Vol 24, pp 311–320

McCorkle, CM, (ed) 1990, 'Improving Andean Sheep and Alpaca Production: recommendations from a decade of research in Peru', The SR–CRSP (Small Ruminant Collaborative Research Project), University of Missouri, Colombia

McCorkle, CM, Brandsletter, RH, and McClure, 1988, 'A case study on farmer innovation and communication in Niger', Communication for Technology Transfer in Africa (CTTA), Academy of Educational Development, Washington

McIntire, J, Bourzat, D, and Pingali, P, 1992, *Crop-livestock Interaction in Sub-Saharan Africa*, The World Bank, Washington DC

Mellor, JW, 1988, 'Agricultural development opportunities for the 1990s – the role of research,' address to the International Centers Week of the Consultative Group on International Agricultural Research, Washington DC, 4 November

Menz, KM, and Knipscheer, HC, 1981, 'The location specificity problem in farming systems research', *Agricultural Systems*, Vol 7, pp 95–103

Merrill-Sands, D, and Collion, M-H, 1992, 'Making the Farmers' Voice Count: Issues and Opportunities for Promoting Farmer-Responsive Research', invited paper presented at the 12th Annual Farming Systems Symposium, Association for Farming Systems Research/Extension, 13–18 September, Michigan State University, USA

Merrill-Sands, D, and Kaimowitz, D, 1990, *The Technology Triangle: Linking Farmers, Technology Transfer Agents and Agricultural Researchers*, International Service for National Agricultural Research (ISNAR), The Hague

Merrill-Sands, D, and McAllister, J, 1988, 'Strengthening the Integration of On-Farm Client-Oriented Research and Experiment Station Research in National Agricultural Research Systems (NARS): management lessons from nine country case studies', *OFCOR Comparative Study* No 1, International Service for National Agricultural Research (ISNAR), The Hague

Miles, DWJ, 1982, 'Appropriate technology for rural development: the ITDG experience', *ITDG Occasional Paper* 2, ITDG

Mills, B, and Gilbert, E, 1990, 'Agricultural innovation and technology testing by Gambian farmers: Hope for institutionalizing on-farm research in small-country research systems?', *Journal of Farming Systems Research Extension*, 1(2), pp 47–66

Moore, WE, 1963, *Social Change*, Englewood Cliffs, New Jersey, Prentice-Hall Inc.

Moris, J, and Copestake, J, 1993, *Qualitative enquiry for rural development: a review*, Overseas Development Institute/Intermediate Technology Publications, London

Mosher, C, 1989, 'Gender planning in the Third World: Meeting practical and strategic gender needs', *World Development*, Vol 17(11), pp 1799–1825

Mosse, D, 1992, 'Community management and rehabilitation of tank irrigation systems in Tamil Nadu: a research agenda', paper for the GAPP conference on Participatory Development, 9–10 July

Mosse, D, 1993, 'Authority, gender and knowledge: theoretical reflections on the practice of Participatory Rural Appraisal', *Network Paper* 44, ODI Agricultural Administration (Research and Extension) Network

Muller, EU, and Scherr, SJ, (comp) 1989, *Technology Monitoring and Evaluation in Agroforestry Projects: an Annotated Bibliography*, International Council for Research in Agroforestry (ICRAF), Nairobi

Norman, DW, 1980, 'The Farming Systems Approach: Relevancy for the Small Farmer, *Rural Development Paper* No 5, Department of Agricultural Economics, Michigan State University

Norman, D, Baker, D, Heinrich, G, Jonas, C, Maskiara, and Worman, F, 1989, 'Farmer groups for technology development : experience in Botswana', in Chambers, R, Pacey, A and Thrupp, LA, 1989, *Farmer First: Farmer Innovation and Agricultural Research*, Intermediate Technology Publications, London, pp 136–146

Norman, D, Baker, D, Heinrich, G, and Worman, F, 1988, 'Technology development and farmer groups: experience from Botswana', *Experimental Agriculture*, Vol 24(3), pp 321–331

Nuijten, M, 1992, 'Local Organization as Organizing Practices: Rethinking Rural Institutions' in Long, N, and Long, A, (eds), 1992, *Battlefields of Knowledge: the Interlocking of Theory and Practice in Social Research and Development*, Routledge, pp 189–207

Ofori, J, Prein, M, Fermin, F, Owusu, D, and Lightfoot, C, 1993, 'Farmers picture new activities', *ILEIA Newsletter*, Vol 9 (1), pp 6–7

Okali C, and Knipscheer, HC, 1985, 'Small ruminant production in mixed farming systems: case studies in research design', paper presented at 5th FSSP Annual Research and Extension Symposium, Kansas State University, October

Okali, C, and Sumberg, JE, 1986, 'Examining divergent strategies in farming systems research', *Agricultural Administration*, Vol 22, pp 233–253

Okali, C, Sumberg, JE, and Reddy, KC, 1994, 'Unpacking the package: flexible messages for dynamic situations', *Experimental Agriculture* (in press)

Omolo, EO, Ssennyonga, JW, Kiros, P and Okali, C, 'Commmunity mapping exercises: an evaluation', report submitted to NRI and ICIPE

Ottenberg, S, 1962, 'Ibo receptivity to change', in Bascom, WR, and Herskovits (eds), *Continuity and change in African cultures,* Chicago University Press, Chicago, pp 130–143

Owens, S, 1993, 'Catholic Relief Services in The Gambia: evolution from agricultural research to community-based experimentation' in Wellard, K, and Copestake, JK, (eds), 1993, *State-NGO Interaction in the Development of New Agricultural Technology for small Farmers: Experiences from Sub-Saharan Africa,* Routledge, London, pp 239–250

Painter, T, Sumberg, JE, and Price, T, 1993, 'Your *"terroir"* and my action "space": implications of differentiation, movement and diversification for the *approche terroir* in Sahelian West Africa', unpublished manuscript

Parkin, DJ, 1972, *Palms, wine and witness: public spirit and private gain in an African farming community,* Intertext, London

Parr, JF, Papendick, RI, and Youngberg, IG, 1983, 'Organic farming in the United States: principles and perspectives', *Agro-Ecosystems,* Vol 8, pp 183–201

Paul, S, 1986, 'Community participation in development projects, The World Bank experience', paper presented at Economic Development Institute Workshop on Community Participation, Washington DC

Pingali, P, Bigot, Y, and Binswanger, H, 1987, *Agricultural Mechanisation and the Evolution of Farming Systems in Sub-Saharan Africa,* The World Bank, Washington DC

van der Ploeg, JD, 1989, 'Knowledge systems, metaphors and interface: the case of potatoes in the Peruvian highlands in Long, N, (ed) *Encounters at the Interface: a Perspective on Social Discontinuities in Rural Development,* Wageningen Studies in Sociology, 27, the Agricultural University, Wageningen, pp, 165–182

Poats, S, 1991, 'The role of gender in agricultural development', Consultative Group on International Agricultural Research, Washington DC

Posner, JL, and Gilbert, E, 1991, 'Sustainable Agriculture and Farming Systems Research Teams in Semiarid West Africa: a Fatal Attraction?' *Journal of Farming Systems Research-Extension,* Vol 2(1), pp 71–86

Pottier, J, 1991, *Representation and Accountability: Understanding Social*

Change through Rapid Appraisal, School of Oriental and African Studies, London

Pottier, J, 1992, 'Harvesting words? – No thanks! Thoughts on agricultural advice and extension work in urban Rwanda', paper prepared for IIED/IDS Beyond Farmer First: Rural People's Knowledge Agricultural Research and Extension Practice Workshop, Institute of Development Studies, University of Sussex, 27–29 October

PRATEC, 1991, 'Agriculture and Peasant Knowledge: Revitalising Andean Technologies in Peru', in Haverkort, B, van der Kamp, J, and Waters-Bayer, A, (ed.), 1991, *Joining Farmers' Experiments: Experiences in Participatory Technology Development,* Intermediate Technology Publications, London, pp 93–112

Pretty, JN, Chambers, R, 1992, 'Turning the New Leaf: New Professionalism, Institutions and Policies for Agriculture', overview paper prepared for IIED/IDS Beyond Farmer First: Rural People's Knowledge Agricultural Research and Extension Practice Workshop, Institute of Development Studies, University of Sussex, 27–29 October

Quiros, CA, Gracia, T, and Ashby, JA, 1991, 'Farmer evaluations of technology: methodology for open-ended evaluation', *Instructional Unit* No 1, CIAT

Rajasekaran, B, 1992, 'Farmer participatory approaches to integrate indigenous knowledge systems and research station technologies towards sustained food production and resource conservation in India', 12th Annual Farming Systems Symposium, Association for Farming Systems Research/Extension, 13–18 September, Michigan State University, USA, pp 154–174

Ravnborg, Helle, M, 1992, 'Resource poor farmers: finding them and diagnosing their problems and opportunities', 12th Annual Farming Systems Symposium, Association for Farming Systems Research/ Extension, 13–18 September, Michigan State University, USA, pp 175–191

Reijntjes, C, Haverkort, B, and Waters-Bayer, A, 1992, *Farming for the future: an introduction to low-external-input and sustainable agriculture,* ILEIA, Macmillan, The Netherlands

Rhoades, RE, 1987, 'The role of the farmer in the creation and continued development of agriculture and systems', Workshop of 'Farmers and Agricultural Research: Complementary Methods'. IDS, University of Sussex

Rhoades, R, and Bebbington, A, 1991, 'Farmers as Experimentors' in Haverkort, B, van der Kamp, J, and Waters-Bayer, A, (eds), *Joining Farmers' Experiments: Experiences in Participatory Technology Development,* Intermediate Technology Publications, London, pp 251–253

Rhoades, RE, and Booth, RH, 1982, 'Farmer-back-to-farmer: a model for generating acceptable agricultural technology', *Agricultural Administration*, Vol 11, pp 127–137

Richards, HC, 1985, *The Evaluation of Cultural Action*, Macmillan and IDRC

Richards, P, 1978, 'Community environmental knowledge in African rural development' in workshop on the use of Indigenous Technical Knowledge held at the Institute of Development Studies, University of Sussex, Brighton, 13–14 April, pp 28–36

Richards, P, 1985, *Indigenous Agricultural Revolution*, Hutchinson, London

Richards, P, 1986, *Coping with Hunger: Hazard and Experiment in an African Rice Farming System*, Allen and Unwin, London

Richards, P, 1989a 'Agriculture as a performance' in Chambers, R, Pacey, A and Thrupp, LA, *Farmer First: Farmer Innovation and Agricultural Research*, Intermediate Technology Publications, London, pp 39–43

Richards, P, 1989b, 'The spice of life? Rice varieties in Sierra Leone', Dept of Anthropology, University College, Hutchinson, London

Richards, P, 1992, 'Rural development and local knowledge: the case of rice in Sierra Leone', paper prepared for IIED/IDS Beyond Farmer First: Rural People's Knowledge Agricultural Research and Extension Practice Workshop, Institute of Development Studies, University of Sussex, 27–29 October

Riches, CR, and Shaxson, LJ, 1993, 'Parasitic weed problems in southern Malawi and the use of farmer knowledge in the design of control measures', Paper presented at conference on Agricultural Research for Development held at Mangochi, Malawi, 7–11 June

Rogers, E, 1962, *The Diffusion of Innovations*, New York, The Free Press

Röling, N, 1986, 'Extension and the development of human resources: the other tradition in extension education', in Jones, GE, (ed) *Investing in rural extension: strategies and goals*, Elsevier, London, pp 51–64

Röling, N, 1988, *Extension Science: Information Systems in Agricultural Development*, Wye Studies in Agricultural and Rural Development, Cambridge University Press, Cambridge

Röling, N, and de Zeeuw, H, 1983, 'Poverty alleviation', final report of the research project *The Small farmer and Development Cooperation*, Wageningen International Agricultural Center

Salas, MA, 1992, 'The cultural dimension of the knowledge conflict in the Andes', paper prepared for IIED/IDS Beyond Farmer First: Rural People's Knowledge Agricultural Research and Extension Practice Workshop, Institute of Development Studies, University of Sussex, 27–29 October

Sandford, RHD, 1990, 'Proposals for a farmers' research project', submitted for funding by Farm Africa, Ethiopia

Sarch, MT, 1993, 'Case study of the farmer innovation and technology testing programme in The Gambia', in Wellard, K, and Copestake, JK, (eds), 1993, *State-NGO Interaction in the Development of New Agricultural Technology for small Farmers: Experiences from Sub-Saharan Africa*, Routledge, London, pp 225–238

de Sardan, J-PO, 1990, 'Populisme développementiste et populisme en sciences sociales: ideologie, action, connaissance.' *Cahiers d'Etudes Africaines*, Vol 120 XXX(4), pp 475–492

Scheer, SJ, 1991, 'On-farm research: the challenges of agroforestry', *Agroforestry Systems*, 15, pp 95–110

Scheidegger, U, Sperling, L, Camacho, L, Nyabyenda, P, Gasana, G, and Buruchara, R, 1991, 'La participation des paysannes dans la selection varietale'. *Actes du Sixieme Seminaire Regional sur l'Amelioration du Haricot dans la Region des Grands Lacs*, Kigali, Rwanda, 12–25 Janvier. CIAT African Workshop Series No 17

Shetty, S, (nd), 'Development projects in assessing empowerment', *Occasional Paper Series* No 3, Society for Participatory Research in Asia, New Delhi

Schneider, HK, 1962, 'Pakot resistance to change', in Bascom, WR, and Herskovits (eds), *Continuity and change in African cultures*, Chicago University Press, Chicago, pp 144–147

Schön, DA, 1983, *The reflective practitioner. How professionals think in action*, Basic Books, New York

Scoones, I, and McCracken, J, 1989, *Participatory rapid rural appraisal in Wollo, Ethiopia: peasant association planning for Natural Resource Management*, Ethiopian Red Cross Society and Sustainable Agriculture Programme, IIED, UK

Scoones, I, and Thompson, J, 1992, 'Beyond farmer first: rural people's knowledge, agricultural research and extension practice: towards a theoretical framework', Overview Paper prepared for IIED/IDS Beyond Farmer First: Rural People's Knowledge Agricultural Research and Extension Practice Workshop, Institute of Development Studies, University of Sussex, 27–29 October

Shetty, S, (nd), 'Development projects in assessing empowerment', *Occasional Paper Series*, No 3, New Delhi, Society for Participatory Research in Asia

Simmonds, NW, 1986, 'Farming Systems Research in the Tropics', *Experimental Agriculture*, Vol 22, pp 1–13

Sperling, L, 1992, 'Farmer participation in the development of bean varieties in Rwanda' in Moock, J, and Rhoades, R, (eds), *Diversity, Farmer Knowledge and Sustainability*, Cornell University Press, Ithaca, New York

Sperling, L, and Loevinsohn, ME, 1993, 'The dynamics of adoption: distribution and mortality of bean varieties among small farmers in

Rwanda,' *Agricultural Systems*, Vol 41, pp 441–453

Sperling, L, Loevinsohn, ME, and Ntabomvura, B, 1993, 'Rethinking the farmers' role in plant breeding: local bean experts and on-station selection in Rwanda', *Experimental Agriculture*, 29: (4):509

Spicer, EH, (ed) 1962, *Human Problems in Technological Change*, Russel Sage Foundation, New York

Stamp, P, 1989, *Technology, Gender and Power in Africa*, International Development Research Centre, Ottawa

Stassart, P, (comp), 1992, *The View of Field Workers: 7 Experiences of African Agricultural Programmes supported by COOPIBO*, COOPIBO, Belgium

Stassart, P, and Mukandakasa, S, 1992, 'Participatory Research and Extension: the Experience of the Agricultural Project Muganza', in Stassart, P, (comp), *The View of Field Workers: 7 Experiences of African Agricultural Programmes supported by COOPIBO*, COOPIBO, Belgium

Staudt, K, 1985, *Women, Foreign Assistance, and Advocacy Administration*, Praeger Inc, New York

Steiner, KG, 1987, 'On-farm experimentation handbook for rural development projects: guidelines for the development of ecological and socio-economically sound extension messages for small farmers', *Sonderpublikatien der GTZ*, Gesellschaft fur Technische Zusammenarbeit (GTZ)

Steiner, KG, 1990, 'Manual for on-farm experiments in rural development projects', *Sonderpublikatien der GTZ* No 248, Gesellschaft fur Technische Zusammenarbeit (GTZ)

Stone, L, 1989, 'Cultural crossroads of community participation in development: a case from Nepal', *Human Organisation*, Vol 48(3), pp 206–212

Stolzenbach, A, 1992a, 'Learning by improvisation: the logic of farmers' experimentation in Mali', paper prepared for IIED/IDS Beyond Farmer First: Rural People's Knowledge Agricultural Research and Extension Practice Workshop, Institute of Development Studies, University of Sussex, 27–29 October

Stolzenbach, A, 1992b, 'Farmers' experimentation: what are we talking about?', *ILEIA Newsletter*, Vol 9(1), pp 28–29

Sumberg, JE, 1984, 'Cultivated fodder trees non-specialized livestock producers', Paper prepared for IDRC *Workshop on Pastures in Eastern and Southern Africa*, 17–21 September, Harare, Zimbabwe

Sumberg, JE, 1991, 'NGOs and agriculture at the margin: research participation and sustainability in West Africa', *Network Paper 27*, ODI Agricultural Administration (Research and Extension) Network

Sumberg J, and Okali, C, 1988, 'Farmers, on-farm research and the development of new technology', *Experimental Agriculture*, Vol

24(Part 3), pp 333–342

Swift, J, 1979, 'Notes on traditional knowledge, modern knowledge and rural development', in *Rural Development: Whose Knowledge Counts?*, *IDS Bulletin*, Vol 10(2), pp 41–43

Thapa, YB, Gurung, BD, Rijal, DK, Neupane, RK, Khadka, RJ, Chand, SP, Tiwari, TP, Bajracharya, B, Gurung, GB, Sherchan, DP, 1992, 'Farmers' participation in on-station research: an effective approach to fine tune the criteria for technology verification in agricultural research', Pakhribas, Nepal

Tiffen, M, and Mortimore, M 1992, 'Environment, population growth and productivity in Kenya: a case study of Machakos District', *Development Policy Review*, Vol 10, pp 359–387

Timsina, D, and Poudel, B, 1992, 'Farmer participatory approach to identifying gender issues in agriculture and forestry related activities in Jhapa, Nepal', 12th Annual Farming Systems Symposium, Association for Farming Systems Research/Extension, 13–18 September, Michigan State University, USA, pp 192–212

Tripp, R, (ed), 1991, *Planned changes in farming systems: progress in on-farm research*, John Wiley and Sons, New York

Tripp, R, 1993, 'Invisible hands, indigenous knowledge and inevitable fads: challenges to public sector agricultural research in Ghana', unpublished manuscript

Tulachan, P, and Batsa, A, 1992, 'Gender differences in livestock production management in the Chitwan District of Nepal', 12th Annual Farming Systems Symposium, Michigan State University, 13–18 September

Uquillas, JE, 1992, 'Research and Extension Practice and Rural People's Agroforestry knowledge in Ecuadorian Amazonia,' paper prepared for IIED/IDS Beyond Farmer First: Rural People's Knowledge Agricultural Research and Extension Practice Workshop, Institute of Development Studies, University of Sussex, 27–29 October

Versteeg, MN, and Koudokpon, V, 1993 'Participative farmer testing of four low external input technologies to address soil fertility decline in Mono Province (Benin)', *Agricultural Systems*, Vol 42, pp 265–276

Vigreux, J-M, Esso-Tsar, A, and Lengue, D, 1991, 'Recherche participative et developpement de techniques agrofrestieres au Nord Togo: etude de cas, la Pepiniere-Douche', Paper presented to CARE International

Villareal, M, 1992, 'The poverty of practice: power, gender and intervention from an actor-oriented perspective', in Long, N, and Long, A, (eds), *Battlefields of Knowledge: the Interlocking of Theory and Practice in Social Research and Development*, Routledge, London, pp 247–267

Waibel, H, and Beaden, D, 1990, 'Farmers as members of research teams', in Cammann, L, (ed), *Peasant Household Systems: Proceedings of an International Workshop'*, Feldafing, DSE

Waters-Bayer, A, 1989, 'Participatory technology development in ecologically-oriented agriculture: some approaches and tools', *Agricultural Administration Network Paper* No 7, Overseas Development Institute (ODI)

Welbourn, A, 1991, 'RRA and the analysis of difference' in *RRA Notes No 14 Participatory Methods for Learning and Analysis*, IIED, London, pp 14–23

Wellard, K, and Copestake, JK, (eds), 1993, *State-NGO Interaction in the Development of New Agricultural Technology for small Farmers: Experiences from Sub-Saharan Africa*, Routledge, London

Whyte, WF, 1981, *Participatory approaches to agricultural research and development*, Cornell University, New York

Whyte, WF,(ed), 1991, *Participatory Action Research (PAR)*, Sage Publications, London

Wood, G, and Palmer-Jones, R, 1990, *The Water Sellers: A Collective Venture by the Rural Poor*, Intermediate Technology Publications, London

Woodhouse, P, 1991, 'Participatory agricultural research and grassroots resource management: what role for for the extension service in Africa?', Paper presented at the Conference on Sustainable Agricultural Development, University of Bradford, December 1991.

Worman, F, Merafe, Y, and Norman, D, 1988, 'Increasing farmer participation in FSR/E: the ATIP experience with farmer testing groups', paper presented at Philippines upland research and extension and training workshop, VISCA, Baybay, June 19–24, Dept of Agricultural Research, Agricultural Technical Improvement Project

Worman, F, Tibone, C, and Heinrich, G, 1989, 'Agricultural Technology Improvement Project (ATIP): 1989 adoption study: Spontaneous technology adoption in farmer groups', *ATIP Working Paper* ATIP WP–34, Ministry of Agriculture, Botswana

WRI, 1990, *Participatory Rural Appraisal Handbook: conducting PRA's in Kenya*, World Resources Institute, Washington, USA

Zadek, S, 1993, *An economics of utopia: democratizing scarcity*, Avebury Press, Aldershot, UK

de Zeeuw, H and van Veldhuizen, L, 1992, *Learning for participatory technology development – a training guide'*, ETC Foundation, Leusden, The Netherlands